BIOGRAPHY AND CRITICISM

General Editors
A. NORMAN JEFFARES
R. L. C. LORIMER

14

JOHN OSBORNE

ALAN CARTER

JOHN OSBORNE

OLIVER & BOYD

EDINBURGH

1969

OLIVER AND BOYD LTD

TWEEDDALE COURT

EDINBURGH I

FIRST PUBLISHED 1969

Acknowledgments

I would like to express my very sincere thanks to Raymond Long and Daniel Godfrind, who in their own ways, have greatly influenced this book.

For permission to quote from the plays of John Osborne thanks are due to the author and to Faber and Faber Ltd.

Acknowledgments are also due to *The Times*, *The Sunday Times*, and *The Observer* for relevant quotations, to *Twentieth Century* magazine for quotations from "That Awful Museum", and to MacGibbon and Kee for quotations from *Declaration*, ed. T. Massachler.

Contents

Drama rests on the dynamic that is created between characters on the stage. It must be concrete and it must be expressed, even if it is only in silence or a gesture of despair. The theatre is not a schoolroom, nor is it, as many people seem to think, a place where "discussion" takes place, where ideas are apparently formally examined in the manner of a solitary show-off in an intellectual magazine. It is a place where people spend much of their time responding nakedly—or failing—to the burden of trying to live, and preparing to die.

John Osborne in *Writers Theatre*

Abbreviated Titles

B.B.	=	*The Blood of the Bambergs.*
B.H.	=	*A Bond Honoured.*
E.	=	*The Entertainer.*
E.G.D.	=	*Epitaph for George Dillon.*
H.A.	=	*The Hotel in Amsterdam.*
I.E.	=	*Inadmissible Evidence.*
L.	=	*Luther.*
L.B.A.	=	*Look Back in Anger.*
P.M.	=	*A Patriot For Me.*
S.S.C.	=	*A Subject of Scandal and Concern.*
T.P.	=	*Time Present.*
U.P.C.	=	*Under Plain Cover.*
W.P.S.	=	*The World of Paul Slickey.*

I

Introduction

> I want to make people feel, to give them lessons in
> feeling. They can think afterwards.[1]

THIS has indeed been Osborne's aim and it is a worthy one.
If he has succeeded then he has achieved a significant
victory. Many people have overlooked this self-
confessed purpose and have misconstrued what his real concern is. By concentrating on the social or political issues
involved in his plays they have obscured his primary intention
of reminding us that we are "thinking" animals and should be
capable of imaginative response. Too much emphasis has been
put upon the inessential and the particular, and so the real
meaning of his work is somewhat obscured. His repetitive
obsessive themes are mistakenly regarded as ends in themselves.
They are not. Osborne would be fully aware of the triteness of
his symbols if they were taken to stand alone. When his heroes
outgrow the structure of the plays which contain them, it is
because their struggle is not limited by their particular relationship in those plays. The heroes and their struggles represent a
more universal condition.

Osborne himself has warned us to beware of clutching at
straws or looking for simple answers when he speaks of the
gibberish promoted by a few words Jimmy Porter used in
Look Back in Anger. Those words were: "there aren't any good
brave causes left". Osborne comments:

> Immediately they heard this all the shallow heads with their
> savage thirst for trimmed-off explanations got to work on it,
> and they had enough new symbols to play about with for
> half a year. . . . They believed him, just as some believed
> Archie Rice, when he said: "I don't feel a thing" or, "I may

[1] John Osborne, "They Call it Cricket", *Declaration*, ed. T. Masschler. London,
1957, p. 65.

I

be an old pouf, but I'm not right wing". They were incapable
of recognising the texture of ordinary despair, the way it
expresses itself in rhetoric and gestures that may perhaps look
shabby, but are seldom simple. It is too simple to say that
Jimmy Porter himself believed that there were no good brave
causes left, any more than Archie didn't feel a thing.[2]

We are warned here to put away our stick-on tabs. Unfortunately far too many quick reactions have hardened into set
opinions about Osborne's work. *Look Back in Anger* affords the
prime example of this quick labelling, for few people paused to
examine the implications of the play before they reached for
their "Angry Young Man" clichés. If one wants to study the
texture of ordinary despair, then the first task is to look at the
total picture, to get some perspective, as well as some insight.
We shall probably lose ourselves by taking the short cut.

A second essential is that we are objective, for literary
appreciation is basically a positive function rather than a
negative one. We cannot take too much account of our own
private sensibilities, or we soon become too subjective. To
remain objective when appreciating the work of Osborne is a
difficult task for his subject matter is highly personal, as is his
approach. He is very much concerned with imaginative
suffering, which by its very nature is a solitary experience and
subsequently likely to evoke a personal response. Osborne's
style is very individual and the questions he poses are seldom
rational or even logically directed. Humanity is rarely so.

Misinterpretation is simple for the communication of feeling
is a complex task. If we read into Martin Luther's fear of the
darkness, an evidence of the playwright's nihilism, then we
begin a process which searches out more examples in other
plays, Bill's "gummy little hole", for instance. Before long we
label Osborne a member of the Continental school of pessimism.
Yet nothing could be further from the truth, for he believes in a
truth which is not to be found in a dark pit. Osborne's work
is an attempt to keep us from Beckett's view of the world
beyond. If his heroes sometimes go to the very edge of the abyss
then it is only to prevent us from falling in. This kind of mis-
representation is arrived at by attributing qualities to incidentals

[2] *Declaration*, p. 69.

which they do not possess. Furthermore, if the incidental is a matter of some personal concern then it is but a short step to a subjective appraisal of the whole. It was much too easy to dismiss Jimmy Porter's anger as some manifestation of his neurosis. What was really needed was a thoughtful inquiry into the reasons for that neurosis.

Dr M. C. Bradbrook, in her book *English Dramatic Form*, is guilty of this type of quick appraisal. She writes of Jimmy Porter:

> This self-pity, his weak impulse to destroy and hurt, complementary to his wife's impulse to throw herself away, are designed to be provocative but they have no particular target. Jimmy Porter is a child casualty of the war before the last—the Spanish Civil War. "There aren't any good brave causes any more" he says in the year of Suez. His torrents of invective are set off by Cliff, the decent Horatio to this Hamlet of the Butler Education Act, and by the Colonel, an honest man of good will, whose Army memories are of military bands in India. The heaviest invective is reserved for the Church. . . .[3]

There is no attempt to understand or explain Porter's pain or position, and factually this appraisal is not even correct, for the heaviest invective is not reserved for the Church. Anyway this misses the point of the religious theme, for Osborne attempts to draw our attention to the fact that the established church and its servants have failed in their task. They are not dealing competently with the problems of today. Jimmy's invective is a plea for more religion, not less, real religion, not the imitation we accept. Thus we can regard Dr Bradbrook's words as not being directed either at Osborne's technical ability or at his attempt to influence us at a value level; they are in fact, subjective words.

One point which has been overlooked by most reviewers of Osborne's plays is how well those plays work in the theatre. It may well be that it is the strength of his own feelings shining through the words of his heroes that gives them their force—but his plays certainly do crackle with electricity. Their impact is enormous. We can never forget the sight of these distraught figures towering above their listeners, shouting their defiance,

[3] M. C. Bradboork, *English Dramatic Form*. London, 1965, pp. 186-7.

yet at the same time begging for our response, our love. Osborne is not concerned with providing answers to their social problems. What he tries to do is to show us the *result* of those problems. His plays present evidence, they do not contain answers. The playwright himself would seem to agree with the dictum that "a dramatist's task is to state what problems are not solve them" for he writes in an epilogue to his play, *A Subject of Scandal and Concern*:

> This is a time when people demand from entertainments what they call a "solution". They expect to have their little solution rattling away down there in the centre of the play like in a Christmas cracker. For those who seek information it has been put before you. If it is meaning you are looking for, then you must start collecting for yourself. . . .[4]

Thus his plays are research into the life and society of today. His characters live out their lives in front of us and we are involved emotionally with them. If Laurie is a middle-aged Jimmy Porter and Pamela a weary Helena, then this is because society reflects the same change in our condition. Osborne by questioning the standards by which we live, extends our knowledge of the way our society functions. A play by him is a statement of facts, useful facts which may encourage human beings to arouse themselves and tackle whatever problems face them. There is profound hope in this attitude. Beckett's shrug of the shoulders is not enough.

Osborne's plays serve to emphasise the dangers we face. The powerful rhetoric of the heroes directs our attention to these threats and is designed to prevent us from becoming machines in a computer-crazed world. Osborne has perceived that herein lies the essence of modern tragedy. In a world where daily human beings take on a closer appearance to machines, he tries to keep us idealists, seeing that tragedy is the defeat of the perceptive man in a world of mediocrity with no place for warmth or purity of emotion. Where in our lives, he asks, is there anything to rouse us to significant action. He has never tried to tell us what there is, but simply to suggest that there is not enough. We must find our own answers, make our own

----

[4] *S.S.C.*, p. 46.

response. What Osborne has done is to give us something to respond to. This is not a negative position, and for those who hold that it is, or that he should do more, he has provided his own answer:

> I can hear all kind of impatient inflections. Well, if your characters only mean what they say some of the time when are we supposed to know what they are getting at? What do you *mean*? How do you *explain* these characters, these situations? At every performance of any of my plays, there are always some of those deluded pedants sitting there impatiently, waiting for the plugs to come singing in during the natural breaks in the action. If the texture is too complex, they complain that too much is going on for them to follow. There they sit, these fashionable turnips, the death's heads of imagination and feeling: longing for the interval and its over-projected drawls of ignorance. Like B.B.C. critics they have no ear at all, or they can never listen to themselves.
>
> I offer no explanation to such people. All art is organised evasion. You respond to Lear or Max Miller—or you don't. I can't teach the paralysed to move their limbs.[5]

This might sound pompous, but it is surely the truth. One responds or one doesn't. Osborne has never directly attempted to cure evils or crusade for rights, but simply to provide experiences, to expose and to amplify, and to let us draw our own conclusions. He has never tried to be a teacher-dramatist in the way that Wesker is, and if his characters seem to be the mouthpieces for his own voice, the message is never dogmatic. There is no sudden salvation. If we can feel something, anything, about the "life" we witness on the stage, then we should have enough imagination to create an answer for ourselves.

What does Osborne regard as the major problem facing us? It is the right to be an individual, to live as one wishes to live in an environment which rarely affords full opportunity to do so. We find it difficult to communicate with one another. If we can communicate then we can personalise this machine-like super self-service society we inhabit. We could gather again the belief that we are "decent" and that there are some values worth upholding. Osborne does not tackle this problem by

[5] *Declaration*, p. 69.

rationally analysing the reasons for our problem. He rarely seems concerned with issues. Nor does he dramatise social questions to work upon our collective conscience. He is not concerned with curing any *particular* social evil. He takes a swipe at many of them with his biting rhetoric, but they do not *essentially* worry him. What does is the breakdown in human communication. The theme of isolation is very important in his plays. His heroes are alone in their awareness of what is wrong, yet they are powerless to change anything for the better. The anger of his heroes stems not so much from the injustices dealt them, as from the strain of knowing how different they are to others, and this because they themselves are still capable of loving. Each of them desperately needs some form of response at an emotionally imaginative level. While we may often wish to shout at them to wake themselves up and stop wallowing in self-pity, we can never question the validity of their plea. They ask to be loved, for themselves, complete with failings and fears, as simple human beings, still capable of giving the affection they so desperately need themselves. Osborne's heroes are visionaries looking forward to some unknown ideal. They can also look back warmly to the settled order of the past. What shatters them and brings so much pain is the indescribable tension of the present, as they are forced to seek out and establish relationships in a society which has not their comprehension.

So in the heroes' desperate captivating rhetoric we hear Osborne's plea for communication. His plays are wordy articulate pieces for he sees "words" as our only hope:

> This is why words are important. They may be dispensed with, but it seems to me that they're the last link with God. When millions of people seem unable to communicate with one another, it's vitally important that words are made to work. It may be very old fashioned, but they're the only things we have left. When I turn that electric light on, I don't know why it works, and don't want to. It's a mystery I'm delighted to preserve. But the verbal breakdown is getting to the point where it's dangerous and nonsensical. I have a great allegiance to words.[6]

[6] *The Observer*, 24 May 1968.

That he has succeeded in using words effectively in the theatre is beyond doubt, yet we should remember that a play is an emotional rather than intellectual experience. Osborne never makes the mistake of using words for their own sake, and his plays certainly burn with emotion, in itself an achievement. When we begin to examine a play as a piece of literature, and we do with Osborne's, then we are in fact saying "this worked well on the stage, let's see why". That is a positive fact and a good starting point.

II

Biography

JOHN JAMES OSBORNE, actor, playwright, and ex-director of Woodfall Films, was born on 12 Dec. 1929 in Fulham, London. His father, Thomas Godfrey Osborne, was a member of the fake genteel middle-class which is a frequent target for attack in his plays. Yet Osborne remembers happy days spent with his father's parents, and speaks sentimentally of his grandfather's definition of a socialist: "a man who does not believe in raising his hat". John Osborne was still a child when his father, a commercial artist, died of tuberculosis after spending years in a sanatorium.

Osborne's mother, Nellie Beatrice Grove, comes from a family of pub-keepers. He tells us something of his mother's family in *Declaration*, where he recalls a boyhood in the midst of a brawling, laughing, drinking, moaning environment:

> My mother's parents were publicans—to be accurate, they managed a succession of pubs in London—until my grandfather lost it all. My mother has worked behind the bar most of her life. She still does because she likes to "be with other people". Her own mother, who is now eighty-four, retired a few years ago on a small pension from Woolworth's. . . .
>
> She is a tough, sly old cockney with a harsh, often cruel wit, who knows how to beat the bailiffs and the moneylenders which my grandfather managed to bring on to her. Almost every working day of her life, she has got up at five o'clock to go to work, to walk down what has always seemed to me to be the most hideous, and coldest street in London. Sometimes, when I have walked with her, all young bones and shiver, she has grinned at me, her face blue with what I thought was cold. "I never mind the cold—I like the wind in my face." She'd put her head down, hold on to her hat and PUSH. The whole family pushed, and whenever they got together for some celebration, there would be plenty to drink, however hard things were: that alone is something middle-class people find

8

difficult to understand or forgive. As a small boy I would be given "a little drop of port", and spit apprehensively always, while my grandfather told me that he would live to see the day when I would be Prime Minister of England. During all this, the rest of the family would be yelling news to each other. A lot of it would be about some illness or other. My grandmother would come in and out of the kitchen, usually picking the wrong moments to interrupt my grandfather. . . . Often if I could escape I would follow her into the scullery and get a slice of the "dinner", some winks, and possibly some story about how my grandfather had spent a weekend with some famous music-hall artist at Brighton. . . . By dinnertime— which meant about two o'clock in the afternoon—the emotional temperature would be quite high. There would be battling shrieks of laughter, yelling, ignoring, bawling, everyone trying to get his piece in. A big celebration would be the worst, like Christmas, when there was invariably a row. Sometimes there would be a really large gathering, and we would all go over to Tottenham, which was the family headquarters. Setting out from London, it was an exciting journey. One never knew what might happen. There would be two or three dozen of us—somebody's brother would have a pint too many at the pub and perhaps hit his wife; carnation button-holes would be crumpled; there would be tears and lots of noise. . . . They "talked about their troubles" in a way that would embarrass any middle-class observer. I've no doubt that they were often boring, but life still had meaning for them. Even if they did get drunk and fight, they were responding; they were not defeated.[1]

Osborne attended state schools until he was twelve, but then, probably at the wish of his father's family, he transferred to a minor public school, Belmont College, in Barnstaple, Devon. If the intention had been to give him an upper-class veneer, it failed miserably for he was expelled at the age of sixteen for slapping the headmaster's face, tit-for-tat. The headmaster, Mr Anthony Reynolds, has retold the circumstances of the incident, and states that the expulsion was more the result of Osborne's repeated jeers about the Royal Family, than the slap. Osborne's own account is "he slapped my face, so I slapped him back".

[1] *Declaration*, ed. T. Masschler, p. 80.

"Leaving" school at sixteen, Osborne tried a series of odd jobs. He wrote copy for various trade journals, such as *Gas World* and *Miller*, and then became tutor to a group of children touring with a repertory company. After six months of teaching English and Arithmetic, the local education authority Inspector arrived and Osborne was once again jobless. He became assistant stage manager to the same company, and even began to act. The next ten years were to be a monotonous alternation of twice-nightly repertory, at two pounds per week, and the dole. His first stage appearance was an evacuee in *No Room at the Inn* at the Lyceum, Sheffield, in 1948. His latest was in his own play *A Patriot for Me*, at The Royal Court in 1965, although he has since appeared in a television play, *Brainscrew*, by Henry Livings. Osborne's stage career has certainly helped his writing, and he seems to have acted competently, for Kenneth Tynan, reviewing *Cards of Identity* by Nigel Dennis, wrote:

> . . . who should turn up, wearing false sabre-teeth and a hairless dome, but John Osborne, ruthlessly funny as the Custodian of Ancient Offices! The Royal Court's captive playwright stands out from an excellent cast.[2]

Of his acting Osborne admitted, after his initial success as a playwright:

> Well, I always enjoy acting, and if I were offered a really good part I'd be tempted. But I've never taken myself seriously as an actor, and neither has anyone else. It would really be a bit self-indulgent to do it any more! Of course when I'm writing I see all the parts being played beautifully by me, to perfection![3]

Whilst he was acting in repertory, he wrote verse which he describes as a useful discipline, and a play, *The Devil Inside*, which was produced in Huddersfield in 1950.

He has been married four times, thrice to actresses, and once to a critic. In 1951 he married Pamela Lane, and though they divorced in April 1957, it was whilst living with her, penniless,

    [2] K. Tynan, *Tynan on Theatre*. London, 1964, p. 49.
    [3] "That Awful Museum", John Osborne interview with R. Findlater. *Twentieth Century*, February, 1961.

on a Chelsea houseboat, that he took the script of *Look Back in Anger* to the Royal Court Theatre. His second wife was Mary Ure, who played the part of Alison in *Look back in Anger*, both in London and New York, as well as starring in the film version. They married in May 1957 and were divorced in 1962. There is one child, Colin. Osborne remarried in 1963; his third wife was Penelope Gilliatt, then film, and later, drama critic of *The Observer*. They were separated in June 1966, and Osborne did not defend the divorce action lodged in June 1967. He married Miss Jill Bennett, cited co-respondent in that action, at Chelsea Registry Office on 19 Apr. 1968. Miss Bennett had previously been married to playwright Willis Hall.

The Royal Court Theatre, and Joan Littlewood's Theatre Workshop, were two new exciting projects in modern drama of the fifties, and with *Look Back in Anger* the former became firmly established. The play was first called *On the Pier at Morecambe*, and Osborne had already hawked it round most London producers, all of whom had rejected it. He was known at the Royal Court where he had appeared as an actor in three productions of 1956, *Death of Satan*, *Cards of Identity*, and *Good Woman of Setzuan*. This might have helped him in getting the play accepted, but it did not help its reception by the critics. Reviewers attacked him as "a ruffian and an intellectual upstart who was doing the unthinkable in the drawing room, threatening the good manners and comfortable illusions of middle-class life". Yet with the play he became one of Britain's leading playwrights, as well as the undisputed leader of what many journalists have been pleased to call "The Angry Young Men". Of this tag Osborne had commented: "it was rather irksome . . . like being called the Walls Ice Cream Man!". It was with *Look Back in Anger* that "The Angry Young Men" phrase really caught on in the mass-circulation newspapers, though the movement had in reality started some time earlier. Some critics refuted the title, thinking it inappropriate. Baiwir, for example, maintained that the dominating note was confusion, stemming from the lack of power to change things. They should, he thought, have been called "Bewildered Young Men", which would have been closer to the truth.

Bewildered or not, *Look Back in Anger*, when it eventually

reached Broadway, in 1957, stirred to life even that traditionally jaded first night audience, with its energetic irreverence and biting rhetoric. The play won the New York Critics Circle Award as the best foreign play of the year. In Britain the play had been an important critical and commercial success. The time was ripe for protest. *Look Back in Anger* expressed that feeling, in public, on the stage, and from there it echoed across the land. With the proceeds of this success Osborne bought his first car. When the licence plates arrived they bore the initials "A.Y.M."

His second play, *The Entertainer*, a similar success, was even more noteworthy in that Sir Laurence Olivier *asked* for the part of Archie Rice, presumably on the grounds of "if you can't beat them join them!". Olivier, in a *Time* magazine interview, expressed his opinion about Osborne:

> I still disapprove of Osborne's social doctrines. But I consider him a highly talented playwright. He has the skill to express the feelings of his characters who are unable to communicate with one another.[4]

Osborne seems indifferent to both the resentment he causes and to the acclaim he has received. Some people feel that he has changed of late and point to the differences in tone of his "famous" letters. They ask one to compare his "Letter to the Philistines" or the "Damn You, England" epistle with his later public addresses:

> My hatred for you is almost the only constant satisfaction you have left me. My favourite fantasy is four minutes or so non-commercial viewing as you fry in your democratically elected hot-seats in Westminster, preferably with your condoning democratic constituents.
>
> There is murder in my brain, and I carry a knife in my heart for every one of you. Macmillan and you, Gaitskell, you particularly. I wish I could hang you all out, with your dirty washing, on your damned Oeder-Neisse line, and those seven out of ten Americans too. I would willingly watch you all die for the West, if only I could keep my own minuscule portion of it, you could all go ahead—die for Berlin, for Democracy, to keep out the Red hordes or whatever you like.

[4] *Time,* 24 Feb. 1958.

You have instructed me in my hatred for thirty years.
You have perfected it, and made it the blunt, obsolete instru-
ment it is now. I only hope it will keep me going. I think it
will. I think it may sustain me in the last few months.

Till then, damn you, England. You're rotting now—quite
soon you'll disappear.

This, the most scathing of his public utterances, is certainly
much more forceful than those of a decade later. In an interview with Kenneth Tynan, published in *The Observer* of 7 July
1968, Osborne answers Tynan's question "Are you a patriot?":

> OSBORNE. A patriot for whom? A patriot for me, I suppose.
> I come out of a generation that grew up during the war, and
> that is what one is. Yes, I'm a patriot in the sense that my
> life only has meaning here, not somewhere else. This sort of
> current spurious internationalism, where people respond to
> one another across nations and continents—it seems to me
> very unreal. I don't know whether my focus is getting
> smaller or my England is getting smaller, but if it is I don't
> make any apologies. I think it is more real, and human.
> TYNAN. *Does it worry you when people attack England as a third
> rate Power with outdated pretensions?*
> OSBORNE. Oh yes. Like Dr Johnson, I think one prejudice
> is worth 20 principles, and I hate the f . . . . . Germans and
> I always will and I believe most people of my generation
> always will. Of course, I wouldn't claim that this was
> entirely rational.

Undoubtedly the tone has changed, and some air of detachment has crept in, but I do not think that we should over
emphasise this. While his disgust seems less scornful, his concern is still very apparent, and his plea for commitment much
the same. Why did the "new society" come to mean no more
than a shiny new "mini" parked outside the house? Osborne
still wishes to draw out attention to what he perceives to be the
evils of society:

> I'd like to see this whole hideous, headlong rush into the
> twentieth century halted a bit.

When Lord Goodman, Chairman of the Arts Council, at a
meeting of the Joint Select Committee on Censorship of the

Theatre (1966), called to discuss Osborne's play *A Patriot for Me*, suggested to him that he might need to take "a caravan of archbishops, of literature and everything else down to the Old Bailey" in order to defend himself if theatre censorship were abolished, Osborne replied: "At least it would have brought it to the public attention".

Osborne has visited Russia, going in a spirit of sceptical sympathy, but he came back angry because the organised enthusiasm made him sick. He went to America in no predetermined state of mind, but on his return he felt London to be very parochial and petty. In America he enjoyed himself because he was not involved. In England his deep feeling for his country and his sense of outrage at its injustices constantly trouble him. This outrage at injustice makes him a socialist by temperament, but he is often furious with the Labour Party, feeling that it has not made people think beyond material issues. In *The Entertainer* Archie Rice paraphrases this sentiment in an anecdote related to his family:

> ARCHIE. There was a chap at my school who managed to get himself into the Labour Government, and they always said he was left of centre. Then he went into the House of Lords, and they made him an honourable fishmonger. Well, that just wraps up Left of Centre, doesn't it?[5]

And in the 1968 Tynan interview, Osborne refuted the idea that the working class could ever run the country, rule by instant rabble having little appeal to him:

> OSBORNE. The working class isn't what it was when I got the hell out of it. The trouble is that history has rather pulled the carpet out from under it. If anything takes over it will be technology, not the working class. The Labour Party has appealed to cupidity, and the appeal has been unanswered by technology.
>
> TYNAN. *Would you say that, in the last few years, you've moved towards a right-wing position?*
>
> OSBORNE. That's what people would say, but I doubt whether it's true. I've always had leftist, radical sympathies. On the other hand, I'm an authoritarian in many ways, simply because of the kind of work I do. If I didn't subscribe to some

[5] *E.*, p. 62.

kind of discipline, I wouldn't be able to do it. In that respect, I'm inevitably a conservative rather than an anarchist. But a lot of left-wing feeling nowadays strikes me as instant-mashed-potato radicalism. It hasn't been felt through and worked through. I find it easy and superficial and tiresome.
TYNAN. *More tiresome than right-wing feeling?*
OSBORNE. Not necessarily, but one always expects more of one's own side. One wants them to behave better and have stronger principles. [6]

Osborne admits to some real influence by three authors, D. H. Lawrence, Jean Anouilh, and Tennessee Williams, thinking that the American post-war playwrights conditioned British audiences for plays which deal frankly with real life. Indeed, Osborne is at his most expansive when talking about the theatre. In a conversation with Richard Findlater, he outlined some of his views:

The big danger in the nineteen-sixties is the formation of a new theatre establishment. That, I feel, is the objection to the National Theatre, where all the safest talents will be busy creating some kind of awful museum. . . . Simply on the basis of one's experience of English life, one knows that it would be the smaller, safer people who would be in charge. . . . There's a danger too, that the Establishment of the nineteen-sixties may try to promote a synthetic version of the really new theatre, with all its teeth drawn. Safe apparently high minded middle-brow plays which make all the gestures but are really not very different from the old Shaftesbury Avenue models. We've seen some of those already: both eyes are on one side of the stag's face, but it's still the same old Landseer product in disguise. [7]

What does Osborne see of merit in the British theatre? What does he want to establish?

. . . the theatre that I most enjoy going to in London is the Mermaid, because the building has all the virtues that one demands of a playhouse. It's comfortable, it's hospitable, it has a simple excitement about it, and you feel that you're in a place that has something to do with the twentieth century instead of being shut up in an Edwardian box. . . .

<hr>

[6] *The Observer*, 7 July 1968.   [7] *Twentieth Century*, February 1961.

One of the best things the English Stage Company has done is to make a new kind of management possible. What do I want for the theatre? First, decent conditions for people to work in, and decent theatres built by architects who know something about it. But what I would like most of all . . . is to see artists in the theatre being allowed to *play* at their work . . . the element of *play* seems to have gone out of life . . . I think we should be all allowed that kind of scope for a complete artistic freedom, so that sometimes we don't have to please audiences or please critics or please anybody but ourselves . . . it's not my job as a *dramatist* to worry about reaching a mass audience . . . if you are going to do what other people think or say you ought to do, it's a waste of time.

Osborne's individuality and indifference to public opinion are well illustrated here, as is his paramount concern with the theatre. Of his own technique, he had this to say:

In my plays I like to establish a kind of remoteness between the actors and the audience, which I only like to break at certain times, and I can do that in the picture frame stage. I don't visualize a picture frame stage when I'm writing. If I think of anything, I think of a theatre that doesn't exist, and that combines the intimacy of the Court with the grandeur of a circus. I'd love to write something for a circus, something enormous and immense, so that you might get a really big enlargement of life and people.

Seven years later Osborne still retains this experimental attitude and seemed quite proud that his plays are not great money spinners, though he has some cryptic remarks to make about some "new developments" in the theatre:

I haven't had a moneymaking play in London for four years, which is why I have to grub around and write films. I've never had a long run, except for *Inadmissible Evidence*, if you call six months a long run. That's as long as I expect my audience to last out, and by that time they're pretty weary and exasperated. The seats are beginning to tip by the end of the fifth month, like they do after the third day in Brighton. If it weren't for all those lovely European theatres and American colleges, I'd make very little. If I ever reach some sort of old age, that's where it'll keep coming from, provided the theatres are still open. Yesterday I got my usual monthly sheet from my agent, and the overseas money from *Look Back*, *The Entertainer* and all those other bits of real estate was far more than I'm earning in England. But that'll dry up when they're all doing these f . . . . . happenings, spraying each other with varnish.[8]

As relaxation from his writing Osborne likes motoring, reading, listening to music, good company . . . and occasionally, television. He claims to be a cheerful alcohol man, stressing wine drinking as a civilised social activity.

On a personal level, Osborne is six feet two inches tall, brown-haired and blue-eyed and today sports a luxuriant fashionable moustache. Tynan has described him as:

A rather impenetrable person to meet: tall and slim, wearing his shoulders in a defensive bunch around his neck; gentle in manner, yet vocally harsh and crawing; sharp-toothed, yet a convinced vegetarian. He looks wan and driven, and is nervously prone to indulge in sudden, wolfish, silly-ass grins.[9]

David Dempsey in the *New York Times* noted that he speaks "a kind of neutral English, somewhere between cockney and the B.B.C., and with a gentle almost tired inflection. He is cheerful, good humoured and honest". These are remarks Osborne would probably take in the same good humour with which he sweetens much of the withering invective of his plays. One of his favourite anecdotes is told against himself. It recalls a fan letter he received whilst in America for the first performance of *Look Back in Anger*. The letter came from a young man in British Columbia. It read:

Why don't you shut up? My mother liked the play. Both my grandmothers are alive. One saw it on television. I think she liked it.

Asked to compose his own epitaph he replied:

Oh, my God. I expect it would be terribly arrogant. Something like: "He never competed with the mediocre." Something rather unattractive like that.[10]

[8] *The Observer*, 7 July 1968.   [9] *Tynan on Theatre*, p. 58.
[10] *The Observer*, 7 July 1968.

III

The Breakthrough

WHATEVER we might say about Osborne's later career, there is no doubt that *Look Back in Anger* was the play which marked the so-called breakthrough in the theatre of post-war Britain. Every book which purports to deal with "modern" theatre contains an appropriate phrase noting the "revolution", and fixes the date of its beginning as 8 May 1956. Kenneth Tynan's words are typical:

> It all came to a head one May evening in 1956 at the Royal Court Theatre in Sloane Square.[1]

Whilst of course it wasn't a revolution of such sudden occurence, Osborne's play did in fact popularise a new type of play and hero. It is necessary to emphasise this turning point, and to go further by stressing that *Look Back in Anger* was much more than just a critical success, it was a commercial success. What was important about the play was the success it enjoyed and the consequences this had on the group of writers who decided that their future lay in drama rather than in other literary forms. More surprising, they found companies willing to stage their works and audiences ready to appreciate them. It became obvious that there was money to be made in this new wave drama. Osborne achieved the initial breakthrough whilst Arden, Bolt, Delaney, Owen, Pinter, Wesker, and others, were waiting to carry the movement through. They had certain beliefs and attitudes in common, although their work is very different. Essentially they were left-wing, disillusioned, and irreverent. To understand how and why the "revolution" came about it is necessary to look at both the sociological and theatrical history of the post-war period.

The fifties were years of gradual consolidation in which, on the surface, little seemed to be happening. Years in which

[1] K. Tynan, *Tynan on Theatre*. London, 1964, p. 54.

18

successive Conservative governments provided "the good life" as the pattern of trade turned in favour of Great Britain, and as those Goverments profited from measures originating from Attlee's Socialist Cabinet of the late forties. If the word austere had been appropriate for that earlier period, so the word "affluent" became the catchword for the fifties. "You've never had it so good" was plastered across placard and pamphlet. Fortunately many young people were querying our standard for the "good life" and their own chance of contributing anything to that life. Not only the young were rebellious. J. B. Priestley found the time and enthusiasm to write an article for *Today* magazine entitled "What is wrong with Britain Today", in which he stated:

> . . . far too many of the men running this country today have the wrong background, the wrong education and training, the wrong outlook. They may be nice, honest, intelligent fellows, but they are no more fit to run an up-to-date Britain than I am to perform in the Royal Ballet. . . . We know vaguely that we are no longer top dogs in the world, but apart from that we don't know what kinds of dogs we are. We are in danger of turning into a *faceless* nation.

Osborne uses the stage as a platform and he repeats this warning in *Look Back in Anger* where his characterisation of Alison's brother Nigel, echoes Priestley's words:

> JIMMY. Brother Nigel? The straight-backed, chinless wonder from Sandhurst? . . . The platitude from Outer Space— that's brother Nigel. He'll end up in the Cabinet one day make no mistake.[2]

Did "the man in the street" care? The average wage rose from £6.8.0 in 1950 to £11.2.0 in 1960. Conservative "freedom from shortage" led to a vast spending spree. Professor Richard Titmuss coined the phrase "the irresponsible society" to describe the situation.

Class remained an obstacle to opportunity and blocked initiative. Bryan Magee observed that ". . . the cachet of being an Etonian and the magic of the Old School Tie could still take the chinless wonder into the highest places".[3] The "Old

[2] *L.B.A.*, p. 20.   [3] B. Magee, *The New Radicalism.* London, 1962.

Boy" network still exercised a disproportionate influence on our affairs despite several years of post-war Socialist Governments. Yet there were signs of change, a questioning spirit was growing and "treasonable" articles were printed and became more numerous:

> It is gone. Empire, forelock, channel and All . . . as the British, shorn of their ships and vast responsibilities, reluctantly realized the world has overtaken them. We are getting out of date like incipient dodos . . . We have reached a moment of catharsis, either we purge ourselves, or inertia will stifle us.[4]

The flail was to come from the "young angries" and, in its most public form from John Osborne's plays. He was the playwright most involved with class and most concerned with changing class structures, or so it seemed. The young looked around and saw very little which raised their hope or enthusiasm. They saw a world in which two "blocs", the Communist and the anti-Communist, glared threateningly at each other. A world where religion had ceased to function as a positive force. In Britain they inherited a society riddled from top to bottom with class barriers and petty snobberies, an establishment still powerfully entrenched, and a royal family still regarded as a British status symbol long after the rest of the world had got tired of even laughing at our pretensions. They lived in a society where in Cyprus, in the middle of the hostilities, Lady Harding could still tell an *Evening Standard* reporter: "I just attend welfare functions. Everyone there is most friendly and charming". She had presumably noticed nothing. Others had. One of those who had was Jimmy Porter: "Pass Lady Bracknell the cucumber sandwiches will you?" he remarks to Helena sitting in her ecstatic little shed at the bottom of the garden, far from the reality of today. Little wonder then that the young were ready to welcome anybody who took up the fight to revise the principles by which we lived. They sought to change the key necessary to open doors, or better, to have no doors at all. The movement, if it could be called anything as definite as that, was in its essence an expression of disillusionment. Many people were fed up, they were bored, and had

4 J. Morris, *The Outsiders*. London, 1963.

little opportunity for *achievement*. They were searching for a world they could believe in, and even get angry at. All they needed was a call to arms. Osborne sounded that call. He did so in the theatre, and from there it echoed round the land.

The reverberation was loud because of the emptiness of the theatre. If we ask ourselves what was happening on the stage in Britain at that time, the answer is, virtually nothing. Sunshine invariably flooded through the open french windows which gave entry to an "incomparable" actress so that she might arrange the vase of flowers and look surprised when the phone rang. In this atmosphere Terence Rattigan reigned supreme with his plays *The Deep Blue Sea* and *Separate Tables*. Graham Greene and T. S. Eliot could be relied upon for a profitable run, whilst Noel Coward and J. B. Priestley were still in evidence but in rather poor form. The most fashionable sector of the stage were the musicals, *Salad Days*, *The Pajama Game*, *The Boy Friend*; and even the surrealist *Cranks* enjoyed long and financially rewarding runs. The "revolutionaries", if this is the correct term, were Christopher Fry, Peter Ustinov, Dennis Cannan, Giles Cooper, and John Whiting. However there were some signs of a revival. The Stratford Theatre Workshop's first West End success, *The Good Soldier Schweik*, was one and the occupation in April 1956 of the Royal Court, Sloane Square, by the English Stage Company was another. This was a new group directed by the late George Devine, with the avowed policy of staging new plays. If these were happy portents for better things to come, there were many less satisfactory omens. The closing of many of the smaller try-out theatre clubs, through lack of support, was one, another was the disturbing lack of new original playwrights. The time was certainly ripe for some form of innovation.

The success of *Look Back in Anger* might well have been a case of the right play in the right place at the right time. Much of the fiction and drama of the period was written with the assumption that the old order of things still reigned supreme. Osborne's success stems from the fact that he knew this not to be true. He managed to find the right vehicle to deliver this message, and with his play, *Look Back in Anger*, he dosed the ailing aspidistras of the English stage with a strong solution of weed killer.

Osborne's own generation responded to his call. They responded emotionally to what was in its essence an emotional plea for commitment. This was what all the fuss was about, for the play itself contained nothing which was violently radical. The play possessed "heat", a glowing emotional fire burned in it. Today the flames have died to a cosy flicker, but in 1956, in the circumstances of that period, they leapt high:

> JIMMY. I may write a book about us all. It's all here. Written in flames a mile high. And it won't be recollected in tranquillity either, picking daffodils with Auntie Wordsworth. It'll be recollected in fire, and blood. My blood.[5]

It seemed that Osborne had ripped out an inner part of himself and tossed it, bleeding, onto the stage. One could not help but feel the anger at the stupidity of society, and the sense of frustration which extended from the stage. A society which could show such utter disregard towards human suffering as was witnessed in Cyprus and Suez, as well as at home. The impact of the play came from its very immediacy of content, and its unparalleled contemporariness. Osborne turned the mood of the time into the forms of the stage. Many people in the audience were able to recognise their own fears and to hear their own words. Jimmy Porter seemed to combine one's awareness of what was wrong, with one's fear of trying to do anything about it. He personified Britain's condition.

It was as if Osborne had grabbed hold of the bedraggled English drama, given it a good shake, and thrust it by the scruff of the neck into the contemporary world of reality. So, in spite of the general theatrical apathy, and the "squeezing" of small repertory companies, drama was again given the voice of the time. A play once more became an expression of the life and feeling of the age from which it grew. That Osborne appropriately caught the mood of his period is well instanced by the opening scene of *Look Back in Anger*, for 1956 was a year in which high rents were extorted, Rachmann-like, from needy tenants in exchange for dingy attic rooms. Such an attic is the

---

[5] *L.B.A.*, p. 54.

setting for *Look Back in Anger* and in that small flatlet live
three people, Jimmy Porter, his wife Alison, and a friend,
Cliff. We know immediately that this is a play which will deal
naturally with realistic problems, problems like the housing
shortage and the injustice which this scarcity caused. Moreover, the play involves us in other ways: as soon as Jimmy
speaks he decries the "posh" Sunday papers noting how even
when discussing the English novel they can make an article
virtually unintelligible to most people simply by writing three
columns in French. We immediately have an example of the
social barrier, the upper class resenting the interest which
might be shown in the English novel by the "common" man—
thus they discuss it in a language only "they" will understand.
Jimmy Porter became a representative of a generation determined to destroy this kind of "injustice". He was a typical
member of a group which was ridding itself of its lethargy and
becoming a class upon which the future of the whole country
might ultimately depend. That the character chosen to
portray this group in the play was painted in such bold strokes
and with such vivid and often crude colour is one of the
reasons why Osborne's play upset so many people. Many felt
that they were about to be set upon and thrust aside by this
brutish rebel who seemed to care little for tradition. They
attributed to him, in addition to this lack of reverence for the
established, a lack of care for value. In this they were wrong.
Osborne, and Jimmy Porter are very much idealists. There is
feeling and love at the back of much that they say. Their
concern is for true value, not misplaced attachment or habit.
Osborne still cares and acts, he has not yet the sense of unreality
which stems from the bewilderment of people who realise that the
middle-class virtues on which we depend are no longer upheld.

> My objection to the Royal symbol is that it is dead; it is the
> gold filling in a mouthful of decay. While the cross symbol
> represented *values*, the crown simply represents a *substitute* for
> values. When the Roman crowds gather outside St. Peter's,
> they are taking part in a moral *system*, however detestable
> it may be. When the mobs rush forward in the Mall they are
> taking part in the last circus of a civilization that has lost faith
> in itself, and sold itself for a splendid triviality, for the

c

"beauty" of the ceremonial, and the "essential spirituality of the rite". We may not create any beauty or exercise much spirituality, but by God! We've got the finest ceremonial and rites in the world! Even the Americans haven't got that.[6]

One may well disagree with the arguments expressed in this statement though I think many would not, but one cannot deny that he is *concerned* with value here. It is important to establish this concern, for otherwise what must often seem to be a series of petulant and petty jibes, would indeed be just that. Osborne is criticised for being angry with everything, for spreading his attack so widely that he cannot in effect be really angry about anything. His characters are mouthpieces for him to make the extensive mixture of points he thinks necessary. It is true that he rarely develops any of these attacks or reasons them out. Is not his major concern the man who feels himself isolated from the rest of humanity? Osborne's grapeshot covers the whole field of petty obstacles which stifle the individual's communication. By showing us the trivialities but not losing himself in them, Osborne is able to magnify his vulnerable and isolated heroes. These men are surely the essence of the theatre, they are rebels, and basically are more interesting than the reasons for the rebellion. Thus his heroes outgrow the structure of the plots, and their words dominate the plays, perhaps they dominate us. A violent push in the back may well get a person from one side to the other more effectively than all the logic in the world. Yet we must remember that there is an intention behind that push, an intention to convince people of the necessity to stand against everything in modern society which belittles the individual, wastes his talents, and prevents him giving full rein to his emotional expression. What Osborne seeks is not to destroy the moral or social order, but to create one which will give back to him a belief in humanity.

Reaction suggests that people still have the means to control their environment and their role in that environment. That people reacted to *Look Back in Anger* has never been in question. This in itself was a breakthrough. People felt, argued, and thought about what they had seen. They did not, whilst still

[6] John Osborne, "They Call it Cricket", *Declaration*, ed. T. Masschler, p. 76.

in the theatre, think about what to do when they left. That in itself was no mean feat in 1956.

Legend has it that *Look Back in Anger* was received unenthusiastically by the majority of critics, and that it was only when Kenneth Tynan went overboard for the play in *The Observer*, that it got moving. This idea was further supported by the fact that it was not until an extract was shown on television some eight weeks after the first night, that it became a financial success. In truth the play received a mixed reception, with the percentages for and against roughly equal. Whilst most critics agreed that this was the kind of play which the English Stage Company *should* be doing, few seemed to want to commit themselves to anything like real enthusiasm. *New Statesman* columnist, T. C. Worsley, thought that as a play *Look Back in Anger* hardly existed, but that in the soliloquies one could hear the authentic new tone of the nineteen-fifties, desperate, savage, resentful and, at times, very funny. John Barber of the *Daily Express* used similar words, thinking it "intense, angry, feverish, undisciplined and even crazy" and strongly emphasised that it was "young, young, young".

Anger was the keynote for Kenneth Allsop who felt that the audience "whacked round the head, came away dazed and in a masochistic ecstasy from the sheer anger of it". Ecstasy is certainly reaction. *The Birmingham Post* was one of the few newspapers to utterly reject the play, stating that if more plays like *Look Back in Anger* were produced, then the "Writer's Theatre" at the Royal Court must surely sink. Unlikely bedfellows, *The Times* and the *Daily Mirror*, also disliked the play, the former feeling that "its total gesture is altogether inadequate", whilst "more than slightly distasteful", summed up the *Mirror's* opinion. Milton Schulman of the *Evening Standard*, expectedly enough, tried to outgun Osborne with his comment that the play aimed at being a despairing cry, but achieved only the stature of a self-pitying snivel: but he too was shrewd enough to note:

> . . . underneath the rasping negative whine of this play one can distinguish the considerable promise of its author. Mr Osborne has a dazzling aptitude for provoking and stimulating dialogue, and he draws character with firm convincing strokes.[7]

[7] *Evening Standard*, 9 May 1956. (See also page 49.)

Philip Hope-Wallace of *The Guardian* thought that whilst the play was by no means a total success artistically, it was good enough to make the choice understandable and that the English Stage Company had got a potential playwright at last. The promising playwright idea was echoed in the *Daily Mail* by Cecil Wilson, when he wrote:

> . . . the English Stage Company have not discovered a master-piece but they *have* discovered a dramatist of outstanding promise: a man who can write with a searing passion, but happens in this case to have lavished it on the wrong play. . . . We can perceive what a brilliant play this young man will write when he has got this one out of his system and let a little sunshine in his soul.[8]

The "sunshine" remark was one which cropped up time and again in the reviews of the play. It is indicative of the state of affairs in the theatre at that time, for few of the critics could accept that Osborne's brand of despair could be the core of any real drama. He had to get the ugliness out of his system, life wasn't like that. The commercial success of the play is a measure of how far they were wrong.

So much for the dailies. On Sunday, 12 May, both *The Sunday Times* and *The Observer* gave the play good reviews. Kenneth Tynan, *The Observer's* drama critic (now Literary Director of the National Theatre), was the first reviewer to completely accept and acclaim the play. It is important to remember that Tynan was *the* critic as far as most of the educated young were concerned, people who in effect, were likely to pay to see the play. His influence in 1956 was disproportionate to that of the other critics. His readers were those to whom the message, if the play had one, would appeal. I wish I had space enough to give the full text of Tynan's review, for I can well remember reading it myself that Sunday morning and experiencing the feeling and enthusiasm Tynan so obviously had for the play:

> The fact that he writes with charity has led critics into the trap of supposing that Mr Osborne's sympathies are wholly with Jimmy. Nothing could be more false. Jimmy is simply and

[8] *Daily Mail*, 9 May 1956.

abundantly alive; that rarest of all dramatic phenomena, the act of original creation, has taken place; and those who carp were better silent. Is Jimmy's anger justified? Why doesn't *he* do something? These questions might well be relevant if the character had failed to come to life; in the presence of such evident and blazing vitality, I marvel at the pedantry that could ask them. Why don't Chekov's people *do* something? Is the sun justified in scorching us?

Osborne's defence seemed to be in capable hands—Tynan realising that here was somebody presenting post-war youth as it really existed. He was prepared to welcome Osborne almost as a saviour:

> All the qualities are there, qualities one had despaired of ever seeing on the stage—the drift towards anarchy, the instinctive leftishness, the automatic rejection of "official" attitudes, the surrealist sense of humour, the casual promiscuity, the sense of lacking a crusade worth fighting for, and underlying all these, the determination that no one who dies shall go unmourned.

Tynan was not blind to the play's faults, noting that it was too long and also had constructional weaknesses: but, emotionally involved with the play (if I interpret his last paragraph correctly), he called his reader to join this crusade for involvement. We had reached the stage of "them" versus "us":

> I agree that *Look Back in Anger* is likely to remain a minority taste. What matters, however, is the size of the minority. I estimate it at roughly 6,733,00 which is the number of people in this country between the ages of twenty and thirty. And this figure will doubtless be swelled by refugees from other age-groups who are curious to know precisely what the contemporary young pup is thinking and feeling. I doubt if I could love anyone who did not wish to see *Look Back in Anger*. It is the best young play of its decade.

If this whole-hearted approval by Tynan did not suggest to the public that something unusual and exciting was happening at the Royal Court, then it is doubtful if anything would have. Yet the play managed to do no better than its predecessors at that theatre, Angus Wilson's *The Mulberry Bush*, and Arthur Miller's *The Crucible*. It was followed by Ronald Duncan's

Don Juan and *The Death of Satan*, as a double bill, and this in turn was replaced by Nigel Dennis' *Card of Identity*. These played in rotation until the early autumn, when *Look Back in Anger* was given a run of ten weeks to fill in until Brecht's *Good Woman of Setzuan* was ready for production. It was not until the eighth week of this spell that "the public" became aware of the play. The reason was simple, an excerpt was shown at a peak viewing hour on television. What Tynan could not achieve, the "telly" did. Takings jumped from £950 a week to £1,300 and in the final week to £1,700. Thus arrived Jimmy Porter to final acclaim as a precocious representative of his age.

In America the play won the New York Critics Award as the best foreign play of the year (1957), and the American critics were for the most part warm in their praise. *New York Post* columnist R. Watts Jr. called the play "a work of distinction and enormous impact which deserved its high British reputation". The influential Walter Kerr writing in the *Herald Tribune* likened the play to "an early October bonfire that lights a real blaze". Chapman of the *Daily News* thought *Look Back in Anger* "the most virile and exciting play to come out of London in a long, long time, something which set the wits tingling". The *New York Times* picked up Tynan's point, emphasising the savagery of the drama and calling it "the most vivid play of the decade".

In Great Britain as soon as he had appeared, Jimmy Porter was hailed as a brother of "Lucky Jim", another "Angry Young Hero" of the fifties. We have only to look at the authors and playwrights who were labelled "Angry Young Men" to see how meaningless this phrase was. Amis, Dennis, Osborne, Wain, Wilson, all suffered the same treatment. Nigel Dennis, writer of the irreligious *Cards of Identity*, affords a good example of the idiocy of this grouping. Dennis, in real life, was a married man over forty, the father of teenage children. Not only were there discrepancies of age and status within the group, there were more important divergencies of literary content. If we compare Jim Dixon and Jimmy Porter we soon ascertain this. Dixon, the anti-hero of Kingsley Amis' *Lucky Jim*, has the same provincialism and cynicism as Jimmy Porter but he has none of Porter's aspiration. Dixon is unemotional and an anti-idealist, he does not seek any form of human commitment, he draws away from involvement. A lecturer at one of the smaller redbrick universities, his anger is limited to the pulling of funny faces behind the backs of those who do him injustices. His frustration is portrayed by an air of detachment, and by an indulgence in alcohol. Dixon has none of Jimmy Porter's "fire in the belly" and is unconcerned with the fate of those around him. He has given up hope, and sees no answer to be found in social or political improvement.

We must not go too far in this argument for there were of course many points of contact between the two "heroes". Both were dissatisfied with the society in which they existed, and each in his own way, rebelled against the traditional codes of that society. "They are scum" wrote Somerset Maugham of the class of state-aided university students to which both Dixon and Porter belong. The "scum" were generally young, left-wing, state-educated intellectuals concerned with the need to be individuals in their own right. They were articulate on the very subjects that the "ruling" classes held dear to themselves: royalty, politics, religion, class, and marriage. There was no real conclusion to their questioning and criticism. They never suggested that they knew the answers to the problems, simply that the answers of the Establishment might well be the wrong ones. There was no programme of social reform. Things might get better, or they might get worse, at least they were not likely to go on being the same. In this context it was hardly fair to ask the public representatives of this movement to provide answers, though many tried; in reality "we", society, had no answer. There was, and is, no authoritative moral tradition to either uphold or protest against.

What was of vital importance in the fifties was that literature and art began to concern all of us again. Experience became as essential as explanation. If that experience was one of despair, then that is what plays or painting should be about. In this context it was irrelevant to condemn the "Angry Young Men" for their irreverence. We should rather have encouraged and applauded their attempt to portray life as they felt it existed, and as they had experienced it. The "Angries" were in a sense necessary ingredients of the period from which they grew, for they drew attention by their very "publicity" to the need to express, by the written and spoken word, a view of life which corresponded to the reality of that life. No one attempted to say what changes were needed. What they did do was to describe the injustice which existed, and to stress, in plain everyday language the desperate need for *some* change. These young men were not prepared to accept what was offered, and were quite right not to do so. The work of the "Angry Young Men" revitalised English Literature because by expressing a conception of how life actually was and by suggesting what that life could possibly be, they rejected a pattern of existence which had become too firmly entrenched in our society. In doing this they pushed us further away from the "self" which dominated our lives. They made knowledge gained through experience an important acquisition. This knowledge and this experience is the "real stuff" of literature.

Osborne has a frontispiece to the reading edition of *The Entertainer*, which I take to be dedicated to Anthony Creighton, his co-playwright of *Epitaph for George Dillon*. It reads:

To A.C.
Who remembers what it was like, and will not forget it; Who, I hope, will never let me forget it—not while there is still a Paradise Street and Claypit Lane to go back to.[9]

This is life as it is lived, yet at the same time it is a plea for change.

[9] *E.G.D.*, Dedication.

IV

Later Impact

WHILE *Look Back in Anger* was the first of Osborne's plays to be performed in London, it was not the first he had written or had produced. In 1950 a play called *The Devil Inside Him*, written with Stella Linden, was produced in Huddersfield. Five years later, at Harrogate, another of his plays appeared, entitled *Personal Enemy*. The most famous of these pre-Porter plays, *Epitaph for George Dillon*, written in collaboration with Anthony Creighton, became Osborne's third London success when it was presented by the English Stage Company at the Royal Court Theatre in 1958.

Osborne's immediate follow-up to *Look Back in Anger* was *The Entertainer*, first performed on 10 Apr. 1957 at the Royal Court Theatre. Tony Richardson was director and Sir Laurence Olivier played the central role of "the entertainer", Archie Rice. The new play did not evoke quite the same violence of reaction as *Look Back in Anger*, but the critics were similarly divided in their allegiance. Kenneth Tynan qualified his earlier enthusiasms a little in his review of the play for *The Observer*:

> Mr Osborne has had the big and brilliant notion of putting the whole of contemporary England on to one, and the same stage. *The Entertainer* is his diagnosis of the sickness that is currently afflicting our slap-happy breed. He chooses as his national microcosm, a family of run down "vaudevillians". . . . Archie is a droll, lecherous fellow, comically corrupted. With his blue patter and jingo songs he is a licensed pedlar of emotional dope to every audience in Britain. The tragedy is that, being intelligent, he knows it. His talent for destructive self-analysis is as great as Jimmy Porter's. . . . In short, Mr Osborne has planned a gigantic social mural and carried it out in a colour range too narrow for the job. Within that range he has written one of the great acting parts of our age.

Archie is a truly desperate man and to present desperation is a hard dramatic achievement. . . .[1]

These views were shared in one form or another, by the majority of the critics who noticed both the similarity between Jimmy and Archie, and that Osborne had provided another strong lead part. T. C. Worsley summed this up in the *New Statesman* when he wrote. "It is the same voice speaking as we heard in *Look Back in Anger*, making the same kind of protest." It was obvious that Osborne was beginning to establish "familiar" ground. Anger was again the keynote to his view of the world. Archie's songs, complete with a nude Britannia as a back-cloth, sounded anew the refrain of *Look Back in Anger*. The basic contradiction in Osborne's work, the atavistic longing for the past, was again present. The colonel, a remnant of Edwardian India, was paralleled by Archie's father Billy, a "left-over" from the good old days of the music-hall.

Osborne's nostalgia was the subject of much attention, and most reviewers mentioned that it was only the old generation who talked sense. John Raymond thought that they were the only people to bring memory of significant life to the madhouse, the play for him was a genuine piece of twentieth-century folk-art, "a grotesque cry of rage and pain at the bad hand history is dealing out what was once the largest most prosperous empire in the world". Archie was blamed for being "a shabby, shallow song and dance man, a blasphemous, lecherous, self-centred heel". Perhaps he had got too close to the nerve centre of the Establishment for Mr Trewin who opined, in the *Illustrated London News*, that the snatches of hymn-singing in *The Entertainer* were deplorably tasteless!

The play had what might be called "incidental" impact, for with the Suez affair still in the air it was certainly topical, with Archie's son Mick, murdered as a hostage. Further interest was stimulated by the fact that Osborne has adopted some form of Brechtian frame-work for the play. The realistic "family" scenes were encased in the epic frame-work of Archie's music-hall turns. Like Brecht, Osborne generalised his smaller parts, concentrating on the central figure of Archie. Yet it would be

---

[1] *The Observer*, 14 Apr. 1957.

incorrect to think of *The Entertainer* as a "Brechtian" play, for Brecht was trying to encourage detached thinking by his alienation structure, whilst Osborne was probably seeking deeper emotional involvement.

In America, *The Entertainer* was not well received. Brooks Atkinson of the *New York Times* thought it a "hollow allegory", whilst it was a "tasteless disappointment" for *Mirror* reviewer, Robert Coleman. Walter Kerr gave the play a mixed report in the *Herald Tribune*, thinking that as a whole it resembled the neon lights that flickered in the background of the set: it was only intermittently brilliant, rather garish and decidedly chilly. Kerr believed that whilst the play had its faults, serious ones, it came to a final image that was truly moving, with an electrifying central performance.

When Osborne's next play, *Epitaph for George Dillon*, appeared many reviewers took no account of the fact that it was a pre-*Look Back in Anger* play, and phrases such as "Osborne's most clinical vivisection *to date*" were bandied about. Briefly, the play relates the story of George Dillon, an actor-writer of questionable talent, who buries himself in a working-class family he despises. It emphasises the dreariness of that life and its inevitability. The "linking" of Osborne and Dillon in the *Spectator's* review was interesting:

> The whole steampower of his writing comes from this identification with his characters. He seems to stand outside himself and say "Look at you, Osborne. Here you are, over articulate, weakly charming, self-centred, rather callous. Your only excuse is talent, and judging by your achievements so far, the chances are you're a phoney". Almost every young man with creative pretensions has said the same kind of thing to himself in the mirror. But few writers since Pepys have dared rip out that part of themselves in words with such blinding candour and frightening honesty![2]

There certainly were the usual "autobiographical" elements in *Epitaph*, but Harold Hobson writing in *The Sunday Times* found the play very significant:

> It is the rarest of theatrical phenomena, a realistic modern drama which is not bourgeois in its underlying assumptions.

[2] *Spectator*, 4 Aug. 1961.

It is like a familiar building caught at an angle which makes it look like something never seen before.[3]

The central character, George Dillon, struck most people as being well rendered, but they were disinclined to sympathise with him, certainly not to the extent that they were prepared to with Jimmy Porter or even Archie Rice. In an article entitled "Unlucky but too Sorry", the *Daily Telegraph* critic explained that as a portrait, George rang true, but as a person with whom one had to spend an evening, and for whom, one supposed the authors expected us to feel sympathy, then he was inadequate.

There was an ambiguity about the play which led Kenneth Tynan to question Osborne's intention. Were Dillon's tears those of a good writer frustrated by the stupidity of the commercial theatre, or were they those of a bad writer who has now the evidence of his limitations?

Epitaph for George Dillon had much the same kind of reception as *The Entertainer* had received when it was presented in New York. In the *New York Times* Atkinson criticised it for being written on a small scale, whilst the *Theatre Arts* editorial summed the play up as a piece whose parts were better than the whole, one that trailed off into ineffectuality without getting into real focus. The play was so badly received by the critics and public alike that after a run of only three weeks it closed at the John Golden Theatre. However, there was some kind of minority movement to keep it alive, and this resulted in a re-opening at 41st Street Theatre. Its second life was equally limited. Henry Hewes commented on this sorry state of affairs in the *Saturday Review*:

It appears that this secret respect plus the rave notices of several minority critics will not keep *Epitaph for George Dillon* from a premature funeral. That the best play of the new season should only run fifteen performances is shocking. But that all of us have so much become the victims rather than the makers of fashionable public opinion that we don't try to fight for what we believe is superior theatre only verifies the play's bitter attack on our comforting and hypocritical pretensions.[4]

Sunday Times, 16 Feb. 1958.   [4] *Saturday Review*, 22 Nov. 1958.

At this stage in his career Osborne attempted to find another means of expression for his views: he left the hostile arena of contemporary life, and did not return to it until 1965, with the play *Inadmissible Evidence*. The new vehicle for his talent was a musical satire, *The World of Paul Slickey*, which, directed by Osborne himself, had its première on 14 Apr. 1959 at the Pavilion Theatre, Bournemouth. The critics were invited but were asked only to report gossip and not to review the show. They *were* to be given complimentary tickets but in fact somehow had to pay. Little wonder then that reviews were few and far between. *The World of Paul Slickey* is regarded, not without reason, as Osborne's biggest critical and commercial failure to date, though one or two of his other plays run close. It was an attempt at social satire, a genre for which Osborne is curiously unsuited. All the obvious targets—the Church, the Government, the Press, the Aristocracy, pop music, blood sports, capital punishment, and success, were duly attacked. More than anything, the show became an outlet for Osborne's private grievance against the Press, as the dedication suggested it well might:

> . . . I dedicate this play to the liars and self-deceivers; to those who daily deal out treachery; to those who, for a salary cheque and less, successfully betray my country; and those who will do it for no inducement at all. . . .[5]

The most apt comment about the show came from the pen of the theatrical correspondent of the *Daily Telegraph*, who, in a rather humorous article, described it as "opening in a blaze of no comment".

A satire is necessarily objective and this is hardly Osborne's strong point, for while his other plays had contained social criticism it was however subjectively expressed. In any event as far as *The World of Paul Slickey* was concerned, a great deal of apparent "criticism" was weakened by our discovery that the priest, Father Evilgreene, was after all not a priest, and that Paul Slickey himself was not such a scoundrel as we thought. The show never reached America.

Osborne's first play for television, *A Subject of Scandal and*

[5] *W.P.S.*, Preface.

Concern, had a complex and involved history before being accepted by the B.B.C. Other television companies had insisted on a degree of re-writing or adaptation to which Osborne would not submit. The companies' protests were probably justified, for Osborne used an alienation technique, presenting the narrative of the play through the words of an ever-present "Narrator". It was more lecture than play, and the independent television companies obviously feared that their audiences would not become sufficiently involved to be interested. This fear was further increased by a disdainful epilogue Osborne attached to the play mocking the masses for demanding a "solution" to be provided by their entertainment. The B.B.C. gave the play as much help as possible with Richard Burton playing the central character, and John Freeman the Narrator. The story itself is interesting: the prosecution of George Holyoake, a Socialist lecturer, who was put on trial in 1842, for stating in reply to a question at a public meeting that he did not believe in God. Holyoake was the last man to be imprisoned for blasphemy in Great Britain.

The play was granted a reception almost as poor as that accorded *The World of Paul Slickey*. Maurice Wiggin wrote in *The Sunday Times* of 13 Nov. 1960:

> I was not surprised to find arrogance and contempt in John Osborne's first play for television, but the last thing I looked to find was dullness. Yet *A Subject of Scandal and Concern* was distinctly tedious. . . . It was a sort of tract, roughed out lamely in the shape of a few undramatic scenes, with a commentator to link them laboriously . . . the account of his (Holyoake's) persecution had no life as a play, the construction was, well, cursory, and the commentator was required to close the proceedings with a typical insult to the patient viewer.

Wiggin had some pertinent remarks to make about Osborne's intention, when he expressed his disappointment at the failure of the play:

> A pity, for our society—any society—needs the elixir of dissent . . . to get a fatty society up off its seat and thinking idealistically, a writer must be able to write, must be *for* something, and must ride his hobbyhorse on a firm rein. Mr Osborne's are running away with him.

Whilst the vast majority of the dailies were equally critical of the play, and on approximately the same grounds, one "quality Sunday" was impressed. M. Richardson of *The Observer*, writing at the same time, felt that his own eager anticipation had not been disappointed:

> ... for it turned out to be an exceptionally good play. It was also one of the most genuinely highminded pieces of uplift to be shown on television for a long time. . . . The remarkable thing was the way Osborne managed to project himself on to this character and give so strong an illusion of reviving the ambiance of the 1840's, while preserving Holyoake's obsessional cussedness. This was a display of dramatic talent of a high order.

For most people, however, it was Osborne's own "obsessional cussedness" which made this venture into television a flop. From his remarks after the event we might well gather it was to be his last:

> What's so boring about television is that it *reduces* life and the human spirit. Enlarging it is something that the theatre can do best of all. That's one reason I'm not interested in writing for television.

Osborne also had some rather damning things to say about the "mystique" of television:

> ... most of the people on the executive level are dim, untalented little bigots. They create a great mystique around the technicalities of television, which are really immensely simple. Anybody with any creative or imaginative sense can easily master them—or ignore them—.[6]

Sentiments hardly likely to endear him to those "untalented little bigots", yet he has since acted on that medium.

What seemed to go wrong with *A Subject of Scandal and Concern* was that once again Osborne's adoption of the Brechtian technique was not whole-hearted. As in *The Entertainer*, there is a frame-work in one convention, whilst the scenes which that frame-work contains are in another. This apparent failure to progress in technique added to the interest aroused by news

[6] *Twentieth Century*, February 1961.

of his next and second historical play, *Luther*, for one wondered whether Osborne would solve the problem.

The historical material in the play was presented in a straightforward fashion. Luther's own words were used whenever possible, and the play was certainly not Brechtian in any extreme way. The narration was briefly announced from the stage during the natural breaks in the action, and Osborne concentrated on the balance between the psychological forces within Luther, and the pressures the monk encountered from the "outside" world. He handled the adopted material well, and the play was hailed as a success by public and critics alike. The late George Devine's prediction, that Osborne's *Luther* would create as much of an impact as *Look Back in Anger*, was realised. The first performance of the play was given by the *English Stage Company* at the Theatre Royal, Nottingham, on 26 Jun. 1961. It was directed by Tony Richardson, and the part of Martin Luther played by Albert Finney.

The critics seemed only too pleased to welcome their champion (as far as the provision of controversial material is concerned). In *The Observer* Tynan described *Luther* as "the most eloquent piece of dramatic writing to have dignified our theatre since *Look Back in Anger*". Hobson too was full of praise in *The Sunday Times*:

> Mr Osborne shows us that he can use ordinary dramatic construction as skilfully as any conventional craftsman. The constant tortures of Luther in his recollections and dreams of childhood are beautifully gathered up and banished in the exquisite final scene.[7]

Alan Brien of the *Sunday Telegraph* did not share Hobson's enthusiasm for the end of the play, thinking that it left one with no attitude about the prosperous married monk pigging it in his palatial nunnery; yet, overall, he thought it "a hammerblow of an evening". Not all the critics were of a like mind. Trewin, writing in the *Illustrated London News*, felt the play was not equal to its pretensions, for Luther, a great figure, had been minimised. "In that much stronger play *Beckett*", Trewin stated, "there is the figure of a Little Monk.

---

[7] *Sunday Times*, 30 Jul. 1961.

Luther comes to us simply as the narrative of a Little Monk in mental and physical pain". Bamber Gascoigne writing in the *Spectator* chose the same parallel but took up the other end of the stick:

> *Luther* is the perfect antidote to *Beckett*! Where Anouilh prettified his tiny piece with endless irrelevant baubles, Osborne grasps his theme in the very first scene and follows it relentlessly through the play without the slightest deviation or distraction. The play offers no analysis of the causes of the Reformation, no explanation of Luther's magnetism, not even the picture of an age. It merely shows one man's rebellion against the world into which he was born, and his search for a personal understanding of life.[8]

Luther in the same way as Brecht's *Galileo*, underlines timeless human problems; and both plays draw contemporary relevance from the lives of historical characters. When *Luther* was eventually transferred to America it was well received. This might be due to the fact that it was the first play of Osborne's performed there with a non-British background. John McCarten, writing in *The New Yorker*, thought that Osborne, "as sinewy a playwright as any practising today", had tackled a tough theme in *Luther* and brought off a *"tour de force"*. *Newsweek* emphasised the universality of the play, the spectacle of an indomitable conscience battling against consecrated rottenness. Of those who criticised, the vast majority concentrated on the same point, that Osborne had based his ideas of Martin's psychological struggles on Erik Erikson's interpretation in the book *Young Man Luther* (1959). This attitude however, ignores the contemporary relevance of the play, and ꞏꞏꞏds Martin as a symbol of that conviction of futility present in so much of Osborne's work. We might ꞏne last word about the play to Noel Coward, who, when ꞏ to say what he thought of *Luther*, is said to have replied: ꞏpous Hieronymous Bosch"!

ꞏlmost exactly a year after the first performance of *Luther*, orne presented a double bill, *The Blood of the Bambergs* and er *Plain Cover*, at the Royal Court Theatre, Sloane Square.

---

[8] *Spectator*, 4 Aug. 1961.

D

The first half of the bill, *The Blood of the Bambergs*, was a satire on a royal wedding and on the mystique of modern royalty as a whole. Fashionable interest was shown in this production, for it was supposed to make some reference to the wedding of Princess Margaret and Mr Anthony Armstrong-Jones. In fact the play was more like a gigantic catherine wheel going off in all directions at once, with sparks never accurate or consistent enough to light any bonfire. Its fire was weakened by the same kind of "reversion" which reduced to ineffectuality Osborne's earlier satire, *The World of Paul Slickey*. Russell, the "stand-in" Prince, is discovered to be of royal blood after all, and so what appeared to be an attack on royalty is hardly that. The only blow which got home was the one directed against the television commentator, as one critic observed, "the play was aimed at the Royal Family, but hit Richard Dimbleby!"

The Times reviewed both plays, feeling that in *The Blood of the Bambergs*, a re-hash of old material, Osborne had gone to the unnecessary pain of lampooning the most over-satirised figure in British broadcasting, adding that the playwright once again had recourse to his obsessive themes, especially negative patriotism. However, for *Under Plain Cover*, *The Times* was full of praise, noting that the play marked a brilliant new departure by Osborne, bringing Genet into England for the first time:

> Ostensibly an attack on press intrusion, it is at its most original in its portrayal of one very private relationship—that of a married couple whose life consists almost exclusively of acting out sado-masochistic fantasies.[9]

Under Plain Cover certainly generated excitement, though one suspects this was indeed due to its strong Genet-like affinities, rather than any intrinsic merit. In *The Observer* Kenneth Tynan admired Osborne's courage both in stating the facts about a sado-masochistic *ménage* and refraining from condemning it. The first half of the play penetrates an area of life rarely discussed, the relationship between a husband and wife who inhabit a fantasy world, wearing various sets of "kinky" clothes which they receive by post, "under plain cover". At one stage the couple rhapsodise on the subject of "knickers",

[9] *The Times*, 22 Jul. 1962.

and it is interesting to note that in this sequence almost every conceivable description is applied to "knickery", including a number of the reviews of Osborne's earlier plays—"This is the most challenging moral issue of our time", or, "the total gesture is altogether inadequate". Unfortunately the play grinds to a shuddering halt with the appearance of Stanley, the "reporter-snooper", whose editor has discovered that the young married couple are in fact brother and sister. The rest of the story simply pads out into a disjointed ill-conceived play what would have been an excellent charade-like sketch. Nevertheless the opening sequences were interesting enough to suggest that Osborne was on the brink of the new direction which was more than necessary at this stage in his career, for, of his last five plays only *Luther*, in the eyes of the public and critics alike, had lived up to the promise shown by *Look Back in Anger* and *The Entertainer*.

Osborne's next play, *Inadmissible Evidence*, first performed at the Royal Court Theatre on 9 Sep. 1964, won the Theatre Critics Award for the best play of the year (1965). Once more, his work was greeted, in Britain at least, with unanimous praise. Bernard Levin of the *Daily Mail* was quite certain:

> . . . in the writing is Mr Osborne's greatest advance yet, for it marries the effortless flow of the dialogue of *Look Back in Anger* with the questing questioning of *Luther* . . . there is no doubt in my mind that it is Mr Osborne's best play to date.[10]

Harold Hobson gave his article in *The Sunday Times*, the headline "John Osborne's Best Play", and went on to say that the play was superbly constructed:

> I do not believe that any language could be too sumptuous to convey the pity and the pathos and the wit and the comprehending compassion of Mr Osborne's best play. Go to the Royal Court, and you will see it.[11]

Strangely enough *The Observer* of the same day, 13 Sep. 1964 arrived at a very different conclusion when Mary Holland, a guest columnist, headlined her review, "Where's all the Anger Gone?" She felt that Maitland, the central character, was simply the playwright's two-dimensional mouthpiece. The

---

[10] *Daily Mail*, 10 Sep. 1964.   [11] *The Sunday Times*, 13 Sep. 196·

other "quality Sunday", the *Sunday Telegraph* warned us not to go to the Royal Court expecting a great timeless drama, but told us that we could find something almost as rare—"an opportunity to touch a revolting, lovable, dangerous, dying human being".

The play opens with a nightmare trial scene, in which solicitor Bill Maitland displays the state of mind to which life has reduced him. His own life is to be his evidence, and unfolded gradually is the story of a man not capable of withstanding the pressures of a society which does not care about the individual. Bill is left finally, on his own. A situation Mary McCarthy has described as the extreme Osborne nightmare. The play was in the "Osborne Contemporary" tradition with a dominant central character, and sketchy minor parts.

Almost as if by an established tradition the play was not well received by the critics when it reached America, though many reviewers did feel that it at least reached for some timeless validity, in itself a change for Osborne, who usually protested about things which could be helped; in *Inadmissible Evidence* the protest is against that which cannot.

John McCarten, *The New Yorker* critic, was fair but negative, noting that the play's faults were "logorrhea and satyriasis". Most Americans thought the play still very British despite its attempts at general universality. They maintained that it revealed the British weariness and desire to sneer at themselves, showing also the split between those clinging to the past, and those worrying about the future. *Life's* article was headlined "Narcissus Spitting at His Image", and as might be expected from this title, Bill was judged to be an implausible dramatic character, much to blame himself for his plight. The only American critic consistently pro-Osborne is Henry Hewes, and he thought *Inadmissible Evidence* one of the great works of the modern theatre:

> An all out theatrical statement, naked and shattering yet ultimately soaring above the desperation it so relentlessly presents. What Mr Osborne has done is to reflect in one stubborn individual's irrational resistance to his time a fierce portrait of our backwardness and our forwardness, both of

which strike him as unsatisfactory. He is not making a
plea for tolerance or corrective action, but as Shakespeare
did in *Lear*, simply and superbly expressing a horrifying nightmare.[12]

Our earlier remarks about "feel now, think later" are relevant.
Hewes, of all the American critics, is the least prone to seek an
answer, and because of this I think he is closer than most to an
honest appreciation of Osborne.

The Lord Chamberlain censored large tracts of Osborne's
next play, *A Patriot for Me*, which Osborne refused to present
without these passages; thus the Royal Court Theatre was
turned into a private club for the play's performance. *A
Patriot for Me*, which had its first performance on 30 Jun. 1965,
describes how a young, able Jewish officer in the Austro-
Hungarian Imperial Army commits suicide after being blackmailed by the Russian Intelligence Service who had discovered
he is a homosexual. The reception it received was mixed, one
or two good notices, some extremely harsh condemnations, and
many "on the fence" opinions. *The Sunday Times* featured
one of the better reviews, Hobson declaring:

> Mr Osborne manages the slow discovery of Redl's peculiarity
> with extreme finesse. His revelation of the insufficiency of
> women to Redl must surely be one of the most difficult and
> delicate feats in modern drama, and it is full of sadness, beauty
> and distress.[13]

The Times was generally complimentary, emphasising that
A Patriot for Me had appeared but a few months after *Inadmissible
Evidence* and that it represented yet another new direction for
Osborne's talent. His work had grown away from the narrowly
personal, without losing its original fire, and this play, like its
predecessors, was spun from his vitals, however detached its
subject matter might be.

Most critics were in some confusion as to how the play should
be interpreted—was it an attack on homosexuality, or a denunciation of a social system which sacrificed an able man?
Perhaps it was meant to be a criticism of that kind of sub-
conscious inner patriotism which prevents us realising our true

[12] *Saturday Review*, 18 Dec. 1965.   [13] *The Sunday Times*, 4 Jul. 1965.

person? Inevitably this confusion produced some marked differences of opinion, and one noteworthy battle between Mary McCarthy and Kenneth Tynan. Miss McCarthy, given the front page of the *Observer Literary Supplement*, was asked for an "outside" view of the play against the background of Osborne's work to date. She posed many questions. Why did Osborne write this? What did he seem to say? Critical of the dialogue, which she thought to be on the level of "I love you, that's why" Miss McCarthy claimed that the play's chief merit was to give work to a large number of homosexual actors or to normal actors who could "pass" for homosexuals. Her only good word was to acknowledge that towards the end of the play there was one tirade of Redl's denouncing the influence of the Spanish, in which Osborne's true voice could be heard. Kenneth Tynan came to the aid of the play the following week in the same newspaper with a personal attack on Miss McCarthy's insensitivity, a refutation of most of her detailed points, and his own contention, that *A Patriot for Me* broke new ground by repudiating loyalty to Freud and loyalty to country, the twin bastions of Western Civilisation. Whilst this kind of exchange certainly added to the play's impact upon the public, *A Patriot for Me* was not a great critical success. Alan Brien of the *Sunday Telegraph* thought that the play, with a little trimming and glossing over of details, could become the basis for an Ivor Novello operetta. He noted Redl's similarity to other Osborne "heroes":

> All his works are tracts for the times. And Redl appears to be another sacrifice on the altar of those demon triplets in John Osborne's theology—the Cold Warrior, the Class Ruler and the Sexual Blimp. He appears not so much a good man, as a *useful* man, distorted, corrupted and eventually wasted because he was not allowed to be himself.[14]

These words would be pertinent to the majority of Osborne's solitary hero figures, but they would not apply to Leonido, the principal character of Osborne's next play, *A Bond Honoured*. This play is very much *not* out of the Osborne "mould". The playwright himself says of it:

---

[14] *Sunday Telegraph*, 4 Jul. 1965.

In 1963 Kenneth Tynan, Literary Manager of the National Theatre, asked me if I would adapt *La Fianza Satisfecha* by Lope de Vega. It was in three acts, had an absurd plot, some ridiculous characters and some very heavy humour. What did interest me was the Christian frame-work of the play and the potentially fascinating dialectic with the principal character. So I concentrated on his development (in the original he rapes his sister in the opening moments of the play without any preparatory explanation of his character or circumstances) and discarded most of the rest, reducing the play to one long act.[15]

In fact this is not strictly accurate for Osborne does keep much of the original. What he alters is the tempo of the action, revitalising both the plot structure and the emotional intensity of the Lope de Vega play. A one-act play presents enormous production difficulties, and when *A Bond Honoured* appeared at the National Theatre on 6 Jun. 1966, it did in fact have two acts, the second being extremely short. In the Osborne play, Leonido has raped both his mother and sister, which he hasn't in the Lope de Vega, and our credulity is strained further by the stylised production, most of the play's actors being symbolically rendered in semi-darkness, with the central character imposing himself upon the story line from the outside as it were. The play attracted little attention. Most dailies ignored it in what was otherwise a crowded week, and the quality Sundays concentrated more upon the production than the play itself. The *New Statesman* summed up the general view of the play when its theatre critic, D. Jones, called the play "a spare ritual, the formalisation of great violence". It was in fact an expression of what might happen to man if he were able to free himself of all his bonds and pursue evil as some form of clinical experiment.

Osborne's latest plays bear a joint title, *For the Meantime*. This suggests both a transitionary stage in Osborne's own development and his sour comment upon the time in which we live. Both *Time Present* and *The Hotel in Amsterdam* are basically portraits of individuals struggling to keep afloat in an ever engulfing tide of meanness.

Time Present which opened at the Royal Court on 23 May 1968 starring Jill Bennett, Osborne's wife, ought to have been

[15] *B.H.*, Author's Note.

a novelty in that she played the part of Pamela, Osborne's first stage heroine. In reality, Pamela, an unmarried, unemployed actress of thirty-four is very much a typical Osborne hero. The sex may have changed, but the dissatisfaction and the disgust are still the same. There is little action in the play. Pamela who shares an expensive modern flat with a woman M.P. pours scorn on everybody and everything around her—politicians, pot, hippies, sex, education, success, the critics, and all things vulgar. The only person she really cares about is her ailing father, Orme, a famour actor of the old school, and when he dies Pamela reacts by drinking quantities of champagne and sleeping during the day. She becomes pregnant by Constance's young lover, arranges an abortion and moves out. Such is the plot. *Time Present* is essentially a conversation piece with the audience Pamela's closest "confidante." The play has the usual Osborne irregularities. Pamela's relationship with her flatmate Constance is contradictory: she seems too wise for arbitrary sexual affairs, and her dissatisfaction seems to stem more from her love for her father and his era than from her own idealism.

The critics treated the play with respect, but seemed rather hesitant to commit themselves without seeing the second half of the bill. Most of them linked the play with Osborne's earlier work. Frank Markus wrote in the *Sunday Telegraph*:

> *Time Present* is not an exhilarating play. John Osborne's plays make their effect not by virtue of their intellectual distinction, nor by their artistry or delicacy of expression, but by their passionate intensity of feeling. His last two plays explored extremes of self-laceration: with this one he comes up for air. It is mild by his standards—and abrasive by anybody else's. It deserves respect.[16]

In general the critics agreed that the playwright's powers of invective had not declined, but felt that his play was cold and impersonal. Once again Osborne had failed to provide his central character with any opposition, a feature Eric Shorter duly noted in the *Daily Telegraph*:

---

[16] *Sunday Telegraph*, 26 May 1968.

. . . as one of Pamela's admirers observes between sips of champagne (and it is sipped all evening), "You treat people as walk-ons". If only Mr Osborne had taken the tip himself and given his eloquent female hero an opponent then we might have had a play of shape and force and compulsion, instead of these monotonous meanderings and their aspiringly smart backchat.[17]

Ronald Bryden was probably the most enthusiastic of the critics, and concluded his *Observer* column:

Still for once Osborne's created a full-length, rounded character which, while able to work off a good deal of his own wit and spleen can't be mistaken for an avatar of himself. Pamela is, herself, sufficiently spikely and pathetically individual to make an impersonal point about the necessity and loneliness of egotism in a society whose only shared values are fashionable trivia. You aren't commanded to like her, only to respect and pity her. Unlike Jimmy Porter, she refuses to pity herself—in this if nothing else *Time Present* is Osborne's most mature, least self-indulgent play.[18]

The Hotel in Amsterdam, with Paul Scofield in the central role, opened on 3 Jul. 1968. Once again it is a conversation piece, and like *Time Present* recalls Noel Coward's showbusiness *"bonhommie"*. The stage is held by six characters searching for an identity lost on the road to success. Yet the play whilst touching upon areas of group feeling and fellowship revolves around a central touchstone, the tragicomic Laurie. The characters are linked together by their subservience to K.L. the all powerful unseen megalomanic film director for whom the men, and one wife, work. The three couples have escaped to Amsterdam for a weekend without K.L.; once in their hotel they sit around discussing his effects upon their lives. They are a sad group and nothing happens but talk, yet it doesn't matter. As in *Time Present* we see lonely dissatisfied people tackle the problem of purpose.

Herbert Kretzner of the *Daily Express* thought the play:

. . . an allegory about the way we surrender our souls to money, power and influence—and to those who wield this armoury with ruthless skill—*The Hotel in Amsterdam* is a compelling and fearful play. . . .[19]

Most critics welcomed it wholeheartedly, the second half of the bill had more than fulfilled their hopes. Harold Hobson enthused in *The Sunday Times*:

> John Osborne's *The Hotel in Amsterdam*, directed by Anthony Page, is the best contemporary play in London: the richest in wit, the most arresting in mood, the most accomplished in performance, and (what is still more important) the most far-reaching and haunting in resonance. If the other plays were ten times as good as they are (and two of them are very good as it is), it would still be the best play in London. . . . It is about fear, the fear, sometimes well founded but more often not, that seizes on people in middle life, when the future no longer seems bright and certain before them. It is about friendship. It is about goodness. No dramatist of our time is more responsive to goodness than has been Mr Osborne ever since his first play *Look Back in Anger*.[20]

This is a cardinal point in any discussion about Osborne for he has been almost alone in the contemporary theatre in tackling the problem of "goodness". His distress at our decline writhes before our eyes in his plays. His latest work is a powerful moral indictment of our God—success. Strangely *The Hotel in Amsterdam* contains fewer jibes than usual though some creep in—about air hostesses, the pill, marriage, effeminacy, and begging relations. Only a handful of critics wrote disparagingly of the play and most of those ended with remarks like "I don't know that I enjoyed it, but I was fascinated and impressed" or "it remains, however, for all its lack of real drama, a strangely hypnotic, amusing and agreeable evening".

Bryden was again Osborne's champion and in a sweeping conclusion stressed that cumulatively with *Inadmissible Evidence*, Osborne's latest two plays:

> . . . add up to an impressive body of work, our most penetrating and truthful portrait gallery of the mean time we inhabit. One's only regret is that the units should be so fragmentary; that the portraits remain a gallery, not a unified scene. If

[19] *Daily Express*, 4 Jul. 1968.   [20] *The Sunday Times*, 7 Jul. 1968.

only Osborne could bring them together in one play, we might have the new "Cherry Orchard" he dreams of.[21]

This is praise indeed, and with *The Hotel in Amsterdam* Osborne seemed to have fully recovered his public appeal after his fall from grace with *A Bond Honoured* , and to a much lesser extent, the eagerly awaited *Time Present*. Taken together his plays *For the Meantime* do certainly suggest that he is on the threshold of some new direction. Frank Marcus in the *Sunday Telegraph* commented with understanding that Osborne:

> . . . has stated that it is time for introspection. Quite deliberately, he stands still and catches his breath. He upholds the virtues of friendship, honesty, propriety, and self-knowledge. They are middle-aged virtues, but that does not invalidate them. Osborne has earned himself a respite, and although his last two plays are far from exhilarating in terms of theatre, they are preferable to silence. I sympathise with his views and understand his condition.[22]

For her performance in *Time Present,* Jill Bennett was voted "Actress of the Year", by the *Evening Standard* Drama Awards Panel. The same critics acclaimed *The Hotel in Amsterdam*, the best new play, and Milton Shulman, drama critic of the *Evening Standard* wrote in that paper:

> "Undoubtedly, 1968 was dominated by the work of John Osborne. Two new plays—*Time Present* and *The Hotel in Amsterdam*—and a successful revival of *Look Back in Anger* firmly established his claim to be among the greatest, if not *the* greatest, of living English playwrights".[23]

An evening at the theatre remains for Osborne an evening of exploration. New ideas and beliefs are to be tested, and where better to do this than on the "imaginative" stage. This drama, extracted from ordinary life, concerns people forced into situations which for them are desperate. Osborne's ability to create situations relevant to our time, and his power to match to these credible characters, accounts for much of his impact. The essence of this lies in his accurate observation of the mind, problems, speech, and gesture of his characters.

[21] *The Observer*, 7 Jul. 1968.   [22] *Sunday Telegraph*, 7 Jul. 1968.
[23] *Evening Standard*, 30 Dec. 1968.

V

The Public Voice

THE division of Osborne's plays into "public voice" and "private voice" was suggested by a provocative article which appeared in the *Observer Weekend Review* of 4 Jul. 1965. Written by Mary McCarthy, and entitled, "Verdict on Osborne", it began:

> Scott Fitzgerald, in his last years, wanted to write a novel about Lucrezia Borgia. Henry James always wanted to write a novel about Napoleon. Kipling's advice to a writer was: Don't do what you *can* do; do what you can't. The modern drudgery of authorship, of turning out year after year a steadily improving brand product, periodically restyled, makes the author, whatever his private character, occupationally a typical member of industrial society, with unimaginative Walter Mitty-like fantasies of a second, more adventurous self. The odd thing about John Osborne is that this boyish self actually writes plays from time to time under the pen name of John Osborne and gets them produced. *Luther* was one, and *A Patriot for Me* is another. Kipling's advice is useful, if taken in moderation. Any writer who follows it will not commit the fault of repeating himself or fall into self plagiarism. Everyone is prone to this fault, and particularly a writer with a distinctive "voice" like Osborne. Such a writer, like a coloratura or a counter-tenor, finds that he is limited to parts of experience, as it were, already written for his voice's range and timbre.

With the latter point I agree, but I cannot accept that *Luther* or *A Patriot for Me* are "private" voice plays. Certainly, they are historical in their setting, but they are very modern in theme. The problems which face both heroes are those which face all minorities. There is a universal contemporary validity in the plight of Luther and Redl, even if the frame-work of both plays is not of today. If we are to group Osborne's plays then it must be according to their essential nature and concern rather than any superficial common denominator.

We may group Osborne's plays by asking ourselves whether or not they are concerned with a solitary figure, lost without purpose in an emotional void. Thus *Look Back in Anger, The Entertainer, Epitaph for George Dillon, Luther, Inadmissible Evidence, A Patriot for Me, Time Present,* and *The Hotel in Amsterdam* fall within the "public voice" group, whilst *The World of Paul Slickey, A Subject of Scandal and Concern, The Blood of the Bambergs, Under Plain Cover,* and *A Bond Honoured,* are "private voice" plays. Objections can of course be raised, for example George Holyoake, the hero of *A Subject of Scandal and Concern,* is surely a solitary figure: but we can justifiably classify the play as "private voice" because in the actual television production the alienation effect of the Narrator was so strong that most of the play's contemporary relevance was strictly limited. Also there is little "Osbornian" dialogue or rhetoric in the play, and it is only in the epilogue that we hear anything of the "public voice". In general, this division of plays into "public" and "private" is both useful and valid. We shall now examine each play in detail, remembering that by illuminating the hostility of repressed groups, they came as disturbing jolts to the conscience of those who could afford to live and let live.

I

Look Back in Anger projected this hostility on the stage, and we know the impact the play had. What we tend to overlook is the idealism behind it. Jimmy Porter was an energetic, vital, young man, but he did not criticise simply for the sake of criticising, behind his anger was a strong desire to establish a better world. His behaviour in the play demanded that the audience questioned values which they blindly accepted as beyond question. Whilst the older generation thought that their beliefs were being savaged, the younger generation felt that at last their opinions were being aired. In other words, *Look Back in Anger involved* people. It did not attempt to provide them with any answers, it conformed to Chekov's dictum that it is the task of a play to state the problem, not to give the solution. Jimmy Porter sought a system of values which would enable him to belong, he was unable to accept the traditional values of his society, and refused to meekly accept his lot, he was determined to break down the cruel insensitivity of "the Establishment". The play was creative in the sense that it made obvious the need for greater opportunity of achievement than that provided by the "irresponsible society" Jimmy found himself living in. He was a human worthy of more than he was offered.

The drab settings of the play serve to emphasise the contrast between the idealistic Jimmy and the dull reality of the world surrounding him. We are never allowed to think that Jimmy may be wrong, only twice in the play does he apologise, once to Alison, whom he burns with an iron, and once to Cliff his friend, whom he allows to leave instead of throwing out Helena, his wife's actress "friend". Jimmy never admits that he could be wrong or that his treatment of others is not fair. Alison certainly does nothing in the play which warrants the venom with which Jimmy attacks her. It is because of his need to establish the ideal of a full unhampered life in the person of Jimmy, that Osborne never allows us to doubt the correctness of Jimmy's actions. He is negative only in that he has no real alternatives to offer.

The central character dominates the other characters and the plot: the play's story-line is a closed circle around Jimmy Porter, an articulate, angry, young man. The anger is less important than the articulation. It is the ability of Jimmy to express himself which saves the play from being parochial, for the social reference of the play is very limited, almost provincial. But we must remember that Osborne is concerned with reality, which to him means the loss of values in our post-war world. We must not become cynical or disillusioned, but fight to discover truth, and to establish better standards which we can then integrate into a practical social system. *Look Back in Anger* was a medium which Osborne used to illustrate the futility and fatuity of most of our established mores and beliefs. If awoken, we might question the validity of our accepted institutionalised beliefs. In the play, Alison's father, a retired Army Colonel, reaches this very point when he asks himself:

COLONEL. Perhaps Jimmy is right? Perhaps I am— what was it? An old plant left over from Edwardian Wilderness. And I can't understand why the sun isn't shining anymore?[1]

Osborne did not intend to force us to this conclusion by the structure of his play, for *Look Back in Anger* is a rather formal three-act play conventionally fourth wall with a one box set. It has strong climaxes, plenty of humorous relief, and it is fairly consistent in style. Only the length of Jimmy's speeches disturb its naturalism. The shock element was to come from the invectiveness and ferocity of the language, and from Jimmy's character, although he is in fact much less committed than he seems to be. The plot is dramatically and chronologically sound if lacking a little in suspense. If it has a weakness it is the rather sentimental ending. Many critics took this to be an implied irony on the part of the playwright for they could not believe, in the light of what had gone before, that Osborne intended this ending to be one of hope. However, director Richardson has emphasised that this was the intention. Alison had suffered sufficiently enough for Jimmy to warm to her, and so a reconciliation could be hopefully effected.

Osborne himself has said that although *Look Back in Anger* was a rather old-fashioned play, he felt that it broke out by its use of language. Most things are admissible so long as they were in character or reasonably funny. The language was in effect provided for one voice only—Jimmy Porter's. The characterisation of the minor parts is only sketchily drawn, the other characters have little independent life at all, they are merely "typical": Alison, the long-suffering wife; the Colonel, an Edwardian relic; Cliff, the faithful friend; and Helena, a bitchy actress. They exist only in relation to Jimmy. It is in Jimmy's character and in his words that the power of the play lies. Other characters have but "fill-in" dialogue, only Jimmy is allowed to explore the field of ideas. The play is tremendously suggestive and evocative, stimulating by implication dormant areas of response to unposed questions. Not that

[1] *L.B.A.*, p. 67.

implication is the only method used, for there are many fiery frontal assaults:

> JIMMY. . . . the injustice is almost perfect! The wrong people going hungry, the wrong people being loved, the wrong people dying.[2]

Jimmy's voice makes us care about England, it makes us uncomfortable by its incessant probings:

> JIMMY. . . . somewhere at the back of that mind is the vague knowledge that he and his pals have been plundering and fooling everybody for generations.[3]

In 1956 we could no longer sit back and let things slide, not if Jimmy Porter had anything to do with it. He touched the nerve ends of our political, social, and religious conventions, yet always in relation to the way in which they affected ordinary people, never in any abstract sense. The setting, events, and the conversation of the play explored how the conditions of that period affected the life of the characters in the play. It was, in some measure, a warning, the criticism implied in it was meant to stimulate us to something beyond the abject acceptance of what is offered. Social problems did not concern Osborne as far as the action of the play was concerned, although they did of course form much of the background. Jimmy Porter was up against something much more claustrophobic, he was battling against inertia, and despaired at the lack of response he saw around him. He is a man of action frustrated because there is nothing left to fight for, and no one left to respond. Jimmy relates the story about his father's dying to his wife when he himself is pleading for human compassion, asking why she seems to care so little about what people are doing to him.

> JIMMY. He would talk to me for hours, pouring out all that was left of his life, to one, lonely, bewildered little boy . . . the despair and the bitterness.[4]

Having given Alison everything, he begs her to respond and grant him the care and affection he so desperately needs. Jimmy cannot bear the thought that he may end his days in the

[2] *Op. cit.*, p. 94.   *Op. cit.*, p. 20.   [4] *Op. cit.*, p. 58.

same way as his father. This is his plea. Is there not something wrong with a society which permits such a death and comfortably goes about its everyday life? Can society make people so unfeeling? It is in this sense that *Look Back in Anger* is a play about people, about human relationships.

The play opens with a scene in which Jimmy and his friend Cliff are sprawled out in their attic room reading the Sunday newspapers. Alison, Jimmy's wife, is standing at the ironing board. The attic is dark and dingy, the water tank is disguised as a table, and we are immediately reminded of the dire housing shortage of that period. Jimmy's first words express his disgust with the snobbish tone of the papers, and we know that this play will be full of biting social criticism even if its main concern is with people. Nothing by way of background is provided but we soon begin to establish the character of the occupants of the attic and the relationships between them. What we need to know of their past evolves as the play progresses. Jimmy tries to draw his wife into the conversation but as usual she is not listening. The animosity between them begins immediately, and the further Alison withdraws the more Jimmy demands response. He appears to have married her for two reasons, for whilst he desires her compulsively, he also sees the marriage as some sort of revenge against the class to which Alison belongs. He can alternatively be very tender and very violent towards her. At one moment when openly needful of her love he tells her:

> JIMMY. There's hardly a moment when I'm not watching and wanting you. I've got to hit out somehow. Nearly four years of being in the same room with you, night and day, and I still can't stop my sweat breaking out when I see you doing—something as ordinary, as leaning over an ironing board.[5]

Jimmy is achingly human with this plea, yet he can be quite vicious and cruel, or so it seems. The darker side of his nature reaches its nadir with his curse to Alison:

> JIMMY. If you could have a child and it would die. Let it grow, let a recognisable human face emerge from that little

[5] *Op. cit.*, p. 33.

E

mass of India rubber and wrinkles. Please—if only I could
watch you face that. I wonder if you might even become
a recognisable human being yourself. But I doubt it.[6]

The last remark is particularly despicable and his wife hardly
deserves such treatment, but we can appreciate how Jimmy
has been pressured by the forces of society to take it out on
Alison. It is her lack of response and affection towards
Jimmy which causes him to treat her so badly—he is unable
to burrow into her love and hide himself from a world which
he finds hostile. Jimmy is neither black nor white, he is
capable of the full range of emotions but no one seems interested.
His disaccord with his wife stems from the fact that he blames
her for a similar lack of interest. Such is Osborne's sympathetic
characterisation of Jimmy that we never feel he is unworthy
of our attention, we can understand his despair but we cannot
comprehend Alison's lack of humanity, or has she too been
beaten down?

We learn that the hero is a redbrick university graduate
who married the daughter of a retired Indian Army Colonel
against the wishes of her family. Because his education did
not provide him with a B.B.C. accent or put him on the Old
School Tie network, Jimmy prefers to run a sweet stall in a
street market with his friend Cliff, who lives with the young
couple in their attic flat. This kind of life dissatisfies Jimmy
and his conversational tone is one of constant complaint as he
launches his aggressive attacks on everything that surrounds him.
Much of the time he gibes at his wife's world and her refusal
to reject her past even though she left it to marry him. S. A.
Weiss writes of Jimmy's battle with his wife in an article for
the *Educational Theatre Journal* (1960):

> Jimmy prosecutes this war against her with all the fury of his
> passion, pain and pride, his hate and hurt. He wants her to
> surrender after suffering and humiliation.

Alison does suffer, for Jimmy, finished with the papers, indulges
in some childlike horseplay with Cliff and accidently knocks
the iron against Alison's arm and burns her. He apologises
but she is in no mood for his "Darling I'm sorry", and tells

[6] *Op. cit.*, p. 37.

him abruptly to get out. The tactful, ever faithful Cliff tries
to smooth things out between them and comforts Alison. She
describes to Cliff the void which has formed between Jimmy
and herself:

> ALISON. I keep looking back, as far as I remember, and I
> can't think what it was to feel young, really young. Jimmy
> said the same thing to me the other day. I pretended not
> to be listening—because I knew that would hurt him, I
> suppose, And,—of course—he got savage, like tonight.
> But I know just what he meant and I suppose it would have
> been so easy to say "Yes, darling, I know just what you mean.
> I know what you're feeling." It's those easy things that seem
> to be so impossible with us.[7]

Alison is unable to react and take the steps which would
probably save her marriage and her husband. She remains
indifferent to both Jimmy's attacks and his pleas, for in being
so, she is able to retain something of her earlier "self" which
annoys and irritates Jimmy so much.

Alison confides to Cliff that she is pregnant but cannot
bring herself to tell Jimmy for fear that he will think she has
betrayed him. He already searches her letters, and complains
of her visits to and from her former friends. The first scene
ends when Alison receives a phone call from one of these
friends, an actress, Helena, who is unable to find digs in town.
Alison invites Helena to stay with them, an offer which incurs
Jimmy's anger, and the scene closes with a typical Osborne
harangue, Jimmy describing his wife as having the passion of
a python, devouring him whole, as if he were some over-large
rabbit.

An accurate microcosm of the play is given in the second
act when Alison describes to her friend Helena, now arrived,
the first few months of her marriage to Jimmy, as being, as if
she had been dropped in a jungle. She cannot understand how
two intelligent people are so savage and uncompromising.
We learn that the couple have never achieved any real understanding, and in answer to Helena's probing questions as to
why she married Jimmy, Alison answers by describing their

[7] *Op. cit.*, p. 28.

first meeting; and how everthing about Jimmy seemed to burn, how the sun shone from his blue eyes, yet even then Alison acknowledges that she realised her fate:

> ALISON. I knew I was taking on more than I was ever likely to be capable of bearing, but there never seemed to be any choice.[8]

This is a good example of "filling in the background" for we see how Jimmy was fighting a losing battle long before the period of the play and also how Alison was resigned from the beginning to being unable to cope. Little wonder then that the present state of affairs had been reached!

Helena urges Alison to leave the "madhouse" or at least to tell Jimmy that she is pregnant, warning her that she must fight otherwise he will kill her—"fight or get out". On his entry Jimmy sails into the girls; he gives a sadistically humorous description of his wedding, then violently slanders his mother-in-law, and ends by ridiculing the girls' intention of going to church. Suddenly, having shown Jimmy in a very black light, Osborne gives us a glimpse of his better side. Poignantly Jimmy relates the story of the lonely death of his father, and how he, Jimmy, had learnt at a very tender age what it was to be angry and helpless:

> JIMMY. I knew more about—love . . . betrayal . . and death, when I was ten years old, than you will probably ever know all your life.[9]

With these words he recaptures our sympathy. Our emotional response is further heightened when Jimmy hears the news that Hugh's mother, an old lady who had once helped him, and whom he loves, is dying. Jimmy wants to go to her and asks his wife to accompany him:

> JIMMY. You're coming with me, aren't you? She hasn't got anyone else now. I . . . need you . . . to come with me.[10]

This faltering plea falls on deaf ears. Alison stands quietly, then turns to Helena with the words, "Let's go". Jimmy is rejected, left to give his love, alone, to an old woman he can no longer help. Ironically he is more alone than he thinks, for

[8] *Op. cit.*, p. 45.   [9] *Op. cit.*, p. 58.   [10] *Op. cit.*, p. 62.

he does not yet know that Helena has arranged for Alison to return to her family. This is a good ending to the scene, and we might note here that each scene in *Look Back in Anger* closes in a similarly effective way.

The Colonel arrives to collect his daughter and surprisingly Osborne is sympathetic in his portrayal of Alison's father. The Colonel does not condemn Jimmy and although he cannot understand his son-in-law's motives, he confines himself to remarking that Jimmy just speaks a different language. He even takes some of the blame upon his own shoulders, thinking aloud that his daughter takes after him in preferring to stay in the middle because it's comfortable and peaceful.

With Alison packed and about to leave, the play develops a new facet when Helena announces that she will not leave with them, for she has an appointment in town the next day and so will stay on at the flat for the night. Our interest is quickened by this twist, and rightly so. Jimmy returns giddy with rage at the fact that he has almost been knocked down by the Colonel "that bastard in his car". He reads Alison's "good-bye" letter aloud. When he reaches the sentence "I shall always have a deep loving need for you", his disgust floods out in a torrent of rhetoric and he warns Helena to keep out of his way unless she wants her head kicked in. Undaunted, Helena tells him of Alison's pregnancy. Jimmy becomes abusive, telling Helena that having just watched someone he loved deeply going through the sordid process of dying, Alison's pregnancy seems unimportant. He is shocked out of his mood of self-pity by Helena slapping his face when he calls her an evil-minded little virgin. Someone has at last responded, and the scene ends with Helena kissing him passionately.

Our feelings towards Jimmy change once again. Where are we now? Is this casual promiscuity permissible? Can Helena provide the sense of belonging he despairs of finding? Let me stress again that it is people we are primarily concerned with. Social and political battles have faded into the background. This is drama, a play about people, and one which will last as such long after the particular sociological issues it raises have been forgotten.

The third-act curtain rises on the same setting as the first, the flat, the two men reading, and a girl at the ironing board, only this time the girl is Helena. She has taken on the unenviable task of caring for Jimmy. The situation has become unbearable to Cliff and he tells Jimmy he must leave. Unable to prevent this departure, Jimmy bemoans his own betrayal of his friend, hating himself for letting a woman bleed him to death and knowing that Helena is incapable of giving him what he wants. In fact Jimmy's friendship with Cliff seems much warmer and real than his relationship with either of the women. Moved by Cliff's decision to leave, Jimmy becomes tender towards Helena, praising her for not demanding things from him. When she tells him she loves him, he answers that she probably does, because she regards him as a Victorian General, even if this particular one is fed up with the whole campaign! He begs that nothing should go wrong, and suggests they go out, get drunk, and come back to make "such love, you'll not care about anything at all". As he crosses the room to call Cliff, the door opens and Alison enters. Yet another dramatic scene ending is effected and Jimmy leaves the two girls to sort things out. Alison has lost her child and has been ill, she seems humbled and apologises for returning. She knows, as we do, why she has come back. She has fulfilled Jimmy's wishes, she has lost her child, she hopes now for her husband's acceptance. When Helena admits to Alison's right to be with Jimmy, it is a mark of Alison's new found awareness, that she tells Helena not to bring out the book of rules, for even she gave up believing in the divine rights of marriage long ago. Alison is not at all outraged by Helena living with Jimmy. Helena however is not willing to fight for Jimmy and tells Alison that she has realised that Jimmy still thinks he is in the middle of the French Revolution and that he will never know where he is or where he's going. She tells Alison that she could not herself forget that "book of rules" and that she believes in good and bad, even if she has tried to forget it whilst living with Jimmy. A weakness of the play is that Helena's behaviour here is rather out of keeping with what we have seen earlier of her character. Feeling guilty at the sight of Alison, Helena leaves, but not before receiving a few scornful lashes of Jimmy's tongue when he returns, for he knows that the situation is too much for Helena's delicate hot-house feelings and treats her departure in much the same way as he had earlier treated his wife's "good-bye" letter.

Jimmy and Alison are left alone to try to establish some kind of peace. At first Jimmy reproaches Alison for not sending flowers to the old lady's funeral, but changes to a more tender tone when he describes their first meeting and how he was enraptured by her relaxation of spirit. Finally he tells her, simply, that whilst he may be a lost cause, he thought that if she loved him it needn't matter. Alison's reply is the one Jimmy has sought from the beginning:

> ALISON. It doesn't matter! I was wrong, I was wrong! I don't want to be neutral, I don't want to be a saint. I want to be a lost cause. . . .

Finally, raising her face to him, she triumphs:

> ALISON. Don't you see! I'm in the mud at last! I'm grovelling! I'm crawling. . . .[11]

Alison's submission allows them to unite *hopefully* in the dream world they have created, where Alison is a gleamingly beautiful squirrel, and Jimmy a strong powerful bear, content perhaps never to really make it as successful human beings in a mundane, futile world.

How long can they remain in that make-believe world we must imagine for ourselves, as we must likewise find answers to the numerous other questions the play poses without answering. That some change was necessary, was clearly implied by Osborne in the play. He created a character who overshadowed both the story and the other characters, a man who by his very force of expression increased the doubt in our minds; and in the play, Jimmy is alone in his awareness of man's problem and his isolation. Jimmy Porter was not satisfied with what he was offered—at any level. He sought for a standard which was worthy of him. The fact that the

[11] *Op. cit.*, p. 95.

scenes ended dramatically should not make us think that the play was situation drama, it was much more concerned with emotional characterisation. This characterisation is centred upon one man. Jimmy is so much the driving force of the play that when he is off-stage the tempo sags alarmingly. Neither does Osborne bother to develop Jimmy's relationships with the others in any depth, using them simply to throw Jimmy into greater relief. The only other character with a consistent viewpoint is the Colonel, and his suggestion that even if his Edwardian values are wrong at least it is better to have some than none at all, weakens Osborne's main thrust. In fact, Osborne displays in his later plays a similar sentimental longing for the established order of the past, and minor characters have little depth, thus the burden of sustaining the plays falls heavily upon the central figures. Fortunately, Osborne's great talent is the creation of magnificent lead parts. Little wonder that these have been played by such actors as Kenneth Haigh, Sir Laurence Olivier, Robert Stephens, Richard Burton, Albert Finney, Nicol Williamson, Maximilian Schell and Paul Scofield.

Jimmy Porter was certainly alive, his caustic invective and his powerful rhetoric full of challenging hyperbole, dramatically captured our interest. His anger became a credo. Here was somebody who demanded our recognition and involvement, however much we hated what he said we could never avoid being affected by his words. A man of his period, he represented a widely spread social group, a group gradually increasing in importance, and more significantly, realising that fact. Jimmy was a contemporary figure, living the problems, and speaking the language of the "fifties". Osborne's greatest achievement in *Look Back in Anger* was that he managed to recreate on the stage the everyday problems of a period and to match to them the right kind of contemporary hero. Jimmy was an articulate young man who expressed in direct colloquial language, easily understood, the feelings of ordinary people when confronted by those problems. The play brought to the theatre a sense of dissatisfaction with the social inheritance we so unquestioningly accepted, and one of the best acting parts of the modern theatre—Jimmy Porter, angry young man.

II

Osborne's second play, *The Entertainer*, with a similarly impressive lead part, afforded Sir Laurence Olivier an opportunity to play his first modern stage role for twenty years. It was the part of the Entertainer himself, Archie Rice, a seedy, second-rate, music-hall comedian. The play may be interpreted at different levels. We may interpret it as a story of self-deceit and self-pity, for Archie is trapped into the cliché of his "family's" existence without acknowledging the fact. An equally valid conception is that the play examines the fortunes of a particular family during the Suez crisis, the lowest ebb in the fortunes of the British Empire. Or we may take an even wider view and regard the play as a symbolic representation of Osborne's obsessive theme, the isolation of man because of his lack of communication with other human beings in a materialistic consumer society. It is, of course, too simple to look at the play from any one of these viewpoints. *The Entertainer* is all of them at one and the same time, and as such, like *Look Back in Anger*, it is a drama of people, an expression and an understanding of their problems and their despair. Like *Look Back in Anger* it is full of self-pity and long bitter speeches. *The Entertainer* has three acts, with each act divided into short scenes numbered like acts on a music-hall stage, with electric numbers lighting up at the side of the stage to tell us which scene we are watching. Thus the action alternates between Archie's music-hall turn and the seaside lodging house where the family live. Archie's stage patter makes apt comment on the condition of his life and Britain's life. His stage monologues are certainly more forceful than those made with his family present. Perhaps Osborne is happier talking directly to his audience than to one or two awkwardly "placed" family listeners.

The Entertainer is one play in which we get a full explanation of the phenomena which appeared in *Look Back in Anger* and which occurs in most Osborne plays—the sentimental longing for an order of things since passed.

Archie's father, Billy Rice, a star of the "good old days" epitomises this concern for the past era, and we sense Archie's admiration for the old man and his success, even though he often speaks brusquely to Billy. Archie's own care about the past or the present is hidden behind his scared swagger and his seedy vulgarity. The deadpan face, the endless affairs with young girls, and his fondness for Double Bass all disguise the fact that whilst he is forced to accept the second rate he is not reconciled to it. Archie longs to be held in the same esteem as his father. His awareness of what human emotion can really mean, witnessed by his softly sung blues when he learns of his son's death, shows us that deep down inside he still cares. The dead eyes, the casually tossed off jokes, the glib music-hall patter, simply cover up the raw nerve ends of his feeling. Archie has left anger long behind, only ironic detachment remains, his professional mask hides his bitterness—he is beyond reach. Archie gains our sympathy in the same way that Jimmy Porter did. He asks for our response to replace the shallowness of those around him. Who responds to Archie? Phoebe, his wife? Hardly, for she needs to visit the cinema two or three times a week to pass the time away; she hates Archie "receiving" his young girl friends but is incapable of doing anything about it. His daughter Jean has her own problems, and when she is not concerned with them, she harshly accuses her father of "trying to escape the pain of being alive". Son Frank opts out of any kind of emotional involvement in much the same way that he was a conscientious objector, and he concentrates on looking after "Number One". We can hardly blame Archie for seeking some relief, even if it is a girl on the kitchen table! Ironically this "release" will only deepen his despair, for Archie, with his back to the wall, is one of those people who can still see the writing on it. His virtues are that he admits that he is a bastard, certainly where his wife is concerned, yet he can be very tender toward her, although he betrays her constantly. He also recognises the need for passion in a cold world; his life is an attempt to find such warmth. We sympathise with him when he is unable to achieve this and the play comes to a final image which is quite frightening, with Archie trooping off-stage towards Phoebe, accepting the comfort he is offered, yet knowing it to be inadequate.

The basis of the play is contained in a speech made by Archie's son Frank, who, when asked by his sister Jean if he would like to go with the family to Canada to begin life anew, replies:

> FRANK. Look around you. Can you think of any good reason for staying in this cosy little corner of Europe? Don't kid yourself anyone's going to let you do anything, or try anything here, Jennie. Because they're not. You haven't got a chance. Who are you—you're nobody. You're nobody, you've no money, and you're young. And when you end up it's pretty certain you'll still be nobody, you'll still have no money—the only difference is you'll be *old*. You'd better start thinking about number one, Jennie, because nobody else is going to do it for you. Nobody else is going to do it for you because nobody believes in that stuff any more. Oh, they may say they do, and may take a few bob out of your pay packet every week and stick some stamps on your card to prove it, but don't believe it—nobody will give you a second look. They're all so bloody busy speeding down the middle of the road together, not giving a damn where they're going as long as they're in the bloody middle![12]

This is exactly what has happened to Archie, he has been passed like a blank hoarding at the side of the road. His response to this harangue of Frank's is characteristic. Ignoring the implications of his son's words he tells Frank to be quiet or he'll wake up the Poles living below. Frank's speech illustrates the various levels of the play. It is an indictment against Archie, a bitter social criticism, and at the same time, an expression of the wider theme of frustration with the increasing meaningless of a life lived in mindless self-absorption.

The existence of these various levels of meaning is emphasised by the Brechtian structure of the play. The real life story of Archie and his family is portrayed in scenes enclosed by a frame-work of Archie's music-hall acts. In these acts, Archie is able to make some general comment about life and about the primary action of the play. The professional Archie is a symbolic expression of the decay of the world:

> ARCHIE. I'm dead behind these eyes. I'm dead, just like the whole inert, shoddy lot out there. It doesn't matter because I don't feel a thing and neither do they.[13]

[12] *E.*, p. 67-8.   [13] *Op. cit.*, p. 72.

The Brechtian frame-work and comment does not add any validity to the everyday action, and it is doubtful whether Osborne was in fact seeking an alienation effect in the Brechtian sense. His subject was an emotional one not well served by a non-involvement technique. However, the play broke away from the purely fourth-wall realistic conception, and as such can be regarded as a structural progression for Osborne: but it remained, like *Look Back in Anger*, a political and social caricature of Great Britain. It gave a view of Britain through the eyes of three generations: Billy, wearied with a life that is not what it was; Archie and Phoebe, mechanically performing accepted routines; and Jean and Frank, bewildered and frustrated by their inheritance. These generations are held together not by family ties but by a common bond of predicament. The predicament that whilst what they have at present is not much good, it is probably a lot better than anything the future will bring.

The first act of the play was kept at a deliberately slow pace, for it was essential that Archie should not be projected as a talented performer, or the family as anything but an ordinary inert group. Jean, the daughter, has unexpectedly arrived home from London and finds only her grandfather, Billy, indoors. Once again the background is filled in as we go along for in the ensuing conversation we learn that Archie is about to put his life "savings" into a road show. Phoebe returns from her "occupational therapy" visit to the cinema, and Jean explains to her how she has quarrelled with her fiancé Graham because she attended a Trafalgar Square rally. The different attitudes of the various generations are explored when Jean talks of her brother Mick fighting in Suez and compares him unfavourably to her other brother, Frank, who preferred to go to jail rather than do his National Service. Billy cannot understand Jean's feeling about the futility of Mick's efforts on behalf of his Queen and Country, her cynicism goes beyond his comprehension.

At this point Archie makes his first appearance in the "family play", although we have seen him in his stage act three times, each vulgarly funny, yet with a pathetic air about them. Archie has heard his patter so often that he has ceased to listen to it himself. He carries over into real life the stage banter and throw away delivery in order to ward off any attack on his integrity. He pokes at the sore spots of our existence with his casual technique, and each thrust is delivered with the same perfect timing as are his corny unfunny jokes. Archie takes Jean's sudden appearance calmly, patronising his family, he first provokes the old man and then quietens him by warning Billy not to wake up their Polish neighbours. At this Billy bursts forth with a typical Osborne caricature:

> BILLY. Don't talk to me about that bunch of greasy tomcats! One Britisher could always take on half a dozen of that kind. Or used to. Doesn't look like it now.[14]

It isn't difficult to recognise the boorish hypocrisy of this statement, yet the tail sting could be sadly relevant. We see again this apparent contradiction in Osborne's portrayal of his "period" characters. Is Billy's attitude meant to suggest he is an irrelevant remnant, or is it supposed to typify an era of significant achievement and appropriate values, especially in comparison with today?

It would be wrong to think that *The Entertainer* consists solely of Archie's flippant patter, for Osborne balances this with some tellingly poignant passages. In one of them Phoebe, morose with gin, suddenly pleads:

> PHOEBE. I don't want to end up being laid out by some stranger in some rotten stinking little street in Gateshead, or West Hartlepool or another of those dead-or-alive holes.[15]

This is a fate which we know is almost certainly waiting her, and Phoebe of course has also realised this. Like her husband, she is trapped in a world without hope. Phoebe is sick and tired of her existence amongst a collection of "down and outs" as she calls them, and we sympathise with her. At a far deeper imaginative level we respond to Archie's despair, an articulate failure of a man reminded by the very presence of Billy that he has himself not been a success in life. Surrounded by people incapable of satisfying his needs, he goes on with the charade of

[14] *Op. cit.*, p. 37.   [15] *Op. cit.*, p. 40.

meaningless existence, unable to admit to himself that he is a
flop in the eyes of the public and himself.

The first act ends with Archie disclosing to Jean, when the
others have gone to bed, that he has had a telegram from the
War Office stating that son Mick has been taken prisoner.
He tries to maintain his jocular vein, but tired and weary his
voice falters and he pleads with Jean to talk to him.

Act Two sees the family discussing the newspaper stories
about Mick, who is now to be released and flown home.
Phoebe is annoyed with Jean who is rather condescending towards her stepmother, and Jean is unable to restrain herself
when Phoebe begins to trot out the supposed virtues of Archie's
successful barrister brother. Jean cannot stand the manner
in which brother Bill patronises the family and she bursts out
to Phoebe:

> JEAN. .... I know exactly how Uncle Bill patted your arm—
> just in the same way he'd wait on the men at Christmas
> when he was in the Army. So democratic, so charming, so
> English.[16]

Archie and Frank join in the argument, though Archie can
hardly stand the thought of listening to his wife bemoaning
her fate. Yet tactfully and tenderly he does, turning his scorn
against society rather than against his wife, when she drones
on about her schooldays and her lack of education. We begin
to realise how many needs there are which can never be satisfied
by material progress. The deepest interests are often those
of which we are not entirely conscious, yet we cannot escape
them. Archie becomes bitter knowing that his wife is about
to tell everybody how brother Bill paid for the children's
education. He kills her punch line by telling them himself, and
then Porter-like, he turns on Phoebe:

> ARCHIE. Nobody ever gave her two pennyworth of equip-
> ment except her own pretty unimpressive self to give any-
> thing else to the rest of the world. All it's given her is me,
> and my God she's tired of that! Aren't you my old darling?
> You're tired of that, aren't you?[17]

16 *Op. cit.*, p. 51.   17 *Op. cit.*, p. 55.

The scene ends with one of the slightly contrived dramatic closures the playwright is so fond of. Phoebe discovers that Billy has eaten part of a cake she had specially bought for Mick's homecoming. Movingly her anguish floods out:

> PHOEBE. Oh, you'll buy another one! You're so rich! You're such a great big success! What's a little cake—we'll order a dozen of 'em! I bought that cake, and it cost me thirty shillings, it was for Mick when he came back, because I want to give him something, something I know he'll like, after being where he's been, and going through what he has—and now, that bloody *greedy* old pig—that old pig, as if he hadn't had enough of everything already—he has to go and get his great fingers into it![18]

This passage is incredibly human and worked stunningly in the theatre, one could sense the welled-up rage and misery of Phoebe from whom fate snatches the smallest satisfaction.

Phoebe tries to persuade Archie to accept an offer from their relations to go to Canada, where he could become a public-house manager. Archie dismisses the idea, and we appreciate that the tragedy of the play is now inexorably set in motion, for Archie has closed the one avenue of escape. A policeman calls at the house to tell them Mick has been killed, and Osborne makes rather melodramatic use of the Suez story here, with the scene ending as the drunken Archie slowly begins to sing the blues. The stiff upper lip has been defeated, the nerve ends of his emotion are exposed, he has forgotten what the human spirit is capable of, he suffers as an artist, he is moved to respond. It is possible, that here, Osborne intended an artificiality of such degrading depth as to destroy our sympathy for Archie, but it is more probable that this is the moment when we penetrate the mask of ironic detachment with which Archie conceals his true feelings. Archie's words are full of that sentimental self-realisation which drinking evokes.

The funeral over, the family put together again the bits and pieces of their life. Jean criticises Archie's manner and morals; refusing to allow him to evade the issue, she condemns him for being like everyone else but worse, because he thinks he can

[18] *Op. cit.*, p. 57.

cover himself by simply not bothering and just waiting for the perks to turn up. Jean is in fact threatening Archie's conscience, forcing him to take part in society, however vacuous it may seem. Jean drags out of the others their plans for the future. Archie had hoped that a new show of his would be financed by the parents of his latest young girl friend, but Billy had told the parents that Archie is a married man, thus the new plan is for Billy himself to return to the stage, the success of the show being assured by the old boy's fame. Jean accuses her father of trying to kill Billy, and indeed the next scene presents the funeral. Jean's ex-fiancé, Graham, has arrived to persuade her to go back with him to London. Osborne describes this class of young man as "well dressed, assured, well educated, their emotional and imaginative capacity so limited it is practically negligible . . . if you can't recognize him, it's for one reason only!" Graham damns himself with his own words about "making a good thing of it" and, "living a decent life". Jean refuses to commit emotional suicide by returning to Graham and prefers to "live" with the family. Act Three is in fact much below the standard of Acts One and Two, for it attempts to incorporate both new characters and sudden plot developments quite arbitrarily, and the play's ending does not grow organically from the rest of the play. It ends with a last glimpse of Archie on stage, his act stretched between two musical routines, entitled "We're All Out for Good Old Number One" and "Why Should I Care, Why Should I Let It Touch Me". Both are sad comments on human life, and we get a final moving image of Archie, alone and defeated, walking slowly off-stage. His own words that life is "like sucking a sweet with the wrapper on" describe what life has been for him. Only occasionally are we allowed to glimpse the real Archie beneath the grinning façade. His laconic bitterness towards his audience makes us think that he still *feels*, that he does carry a dream of success. Archie hopes desperately that he will fulfil his wishes, he knows what life could be: "Billy knows, he's heard them singing".

There is a substantial amount of social criticism which we should not overlook, Jean's thoughts being particularly provocative:

JEAN. Why do people like us sit here, and just lap it all up, why do boys die, or stoke boilers, why do we pick up these things, what are we hoping to get out of it, what's it all in aid of—is it really just for the sake of a gloved hand waving at you from a golden coach?[19]

Osborne hints that it is Jean's energy and Frank's anger which will eventually win through, but in the play it is Archie's plight which captures our attention. He mirrors the situation we have reached, his reflection should frighten us into a reconsideration of our values, lest we should end as he does. The play shows the need for a standard of behaviour which would allow people to function properly as *human beings* in a world of common shared belief. Our final impression of the play is the memory of this lonely man, his genuine pain, and his weary acceptance of a deadening existence.

III

Epitaph for George Dillon is regarded by many people as Osborne's most satisfactory play. It is certainly much more balanced than any other work, and the central character is provided with some opposition, however dogged his self-confidence may be, for whilst the Elliot family are two-dimensional caricatures, Ruth, the aunt, does exist on the same level as George, the central character.

George Dillon is an unsuccessful actor and writer who suffers the ultimate ignominy of being trapped into the giant cliché of the Elliot "family", and what is worse, earns their admiration. George is "adopted" by Mrs Elliot as a substitute for her own son of the same age, killed in the war. The Elliot family are the epitome of all that George detests, yet he is content to sponge off them. Mrs Elliot is possessive and sentimental, and her husband Percy, battered into submission, is almost a lodger in the house. His one delight is to make others as miserable as himself. They have two daughters, the eldest, Norah, dull and colourless, and Josie, a selfish, petulant teenager, nobody's fool. The household is completed by Ruth, Mrs Elliot's younger sister, an attractive woman of

[19] *Op. cit.*, p. 78.

F

high calibre but one who lacks the courage to extract herself
from the family and her circumstances. The play is a classic
modern day tragedy—the decline and fall of a worthless man
in an overregulated but vacuous society. George Dillon has
kidded himself for years that he is the real thing, an artist, and
we see him gradually become aware of his self-deception. He
questions the fact that it might be possible to have the conventional pains and doubtings yet not be the real thing:

> GEORGE. . . . the same symptoms as talent, the pain, the ugly
> swellings the lot—but never knowing whether or not the
> diagnosis is correct. Do you think there may be some kind of
> euthanasia for that? Could you kill it by burying yourself
> here—for good?[20]

The play describes how George attempts this burial by marrying
Josie, at the same time becoming commercially successful by
"dirtying" up one of his plays.

We can see the universal validity of George's tragedy. He
is a luckless man, whose selfishness has contributed to his
plight. The play is part of Osborne's theme against the danger
of talented *creative* artists being swallowed up in a world of
debased commercialism. Like Jimmy Porter, George Dillon
is rebellious and homeless; lacking loyalty and hope, life has
become a caricature. George repeatedly rails out against the
Elliots, shaking his fist at the plaster ducks on the wall, "those
bloody birds", yet he is desperately conscious that he may
become just such a caricature. His tragedy is that he is aware
of the situation. In the family, only Ruth has this perception.
She has already accepted her "euthanasia", as she admits to
George in a telling exchange between them:

> RUTH. There's not much else I can do. Perhaps I haven't
> got the courage to try. At least, I'm safe.[21]

Ruth, in her turn, forces George to examine the reasons why
he has stuck like a leech to the Elliots. He goes beyond his
usual superficial self-dramatisation and admits that it is a
temptation to live with the family, rather than an expedient
measure. There he is never questioned, he meets no real

[20] *E.G.D.*, p. 62.   [21] *Op. cit.*, p. 60.

hostility, he needs no imagination. The scene in which George and Ruth probe each other's sensibilities is extremely convincing, and achieves a clear insight into the lives and thoughts of both.

Epitaph for George Dillon has a slow, awkward opening, we are "dropped in" as usual but a lot of time is spent filling in the background to George's long awaited arrival. While we certainly learn something of the various characters in the play the plot makes little progress. The "naturalness" of the set reinforces the static nature of the beginning of the play. It is not until George arrives that the movement of the play begins, and even then the characterisation is more like caricature. In Act Two, for example, Josie remarks:

> JOSIE. S-E-X? Oh, sex. Sex doesn't mean a thing to me. To my way of thinking, love is the most important and beautiful thing in the world and that's got nothing to do with sex.[22]

Of course, by representing the minor characters in this way, Osborne heightens the sense of George's isolation in this jungle of clichés.

George brings home a bottle of wine to celebrate the fact that he has found a small part in a play to be produced in Bayswater and the promise of an appearance on television. The family chatter is disturbed by the entrance of Mr Colwyn-Stuart who comes to escort Mrs Elliot to a religious meeting. Colwyn-Stuart delivers a stereotyped moral lecture to George who unfortunately is provoked to answer the claims of the "shining lights of the soul", with the words:

> GEORGE. . . . life isn't simple, and, if you've any brains in your head at all, it's frankly a pain in the arse . . . I don't care who it is—you or anyone—you must have a secret doubt somewhere. You know that the only reason you do believe in these things is because they *are* comforting.[23]

Osborne expresses here his dissatisfaction with what we accept today as religion. Religion in his sense has abdicated its central position in the scheme of things, and is concerned now

[22] *Op. cit.*, p. 38.   [23] *Op. cit.*, p. 47-8.

with providing comfort. Its position has been filled by the substitute religions of nationalism, politics, and commercialism. Human beings seem to have lost the traditional objects of their belief, but not their habit of believing. Osborne is concerned with man as an individual, an individual with a conscience which needs satisfying, and satisfying by a belief in this world. He does not accept the view that the totalitarianism of the world has produced something too big for us to understand.

The scene between George and Ruth, when Colwyn-Stuart and Mrs Elliot leave, is a lesson in compressed, meaty, dramatic writing, as the two "opponents" force each other to reveal their secret doubts:

> RUTH. Oh don't look like that, for God's sake. You make me feel as though I'm setting up as a soup kitchen or something. Please.[24]

Ruth has already played this role to another untalented young writer, and aware of her suitability for the part she tries to hide her apathy. George forces her to recognise the truth about her existence, to admit to her helplessness and lack of courage. Ruth in turn, makes George accept the fact that the only excuse for his bad behaviour is talent, which he doubts. George admits that he longs to have the disease of talent, however sick it might make him: but when Ruth begs him to save himself and leave the family, he turns the question against her, and demands to know why she still lives there with people who must drive her mad with their lack of curiosity, their lack of questions, and their existence without laughter, without the very essence of life. George's soliloquy is perfectly contained within the action of the dialogue, and the connexion between the author's general theme, and his particular concern with George, is beautifully effected. Ironically Dillon's answer to the question of being alive will be to seek a living death with the Elliots. He can no longer tell what is real and what isn't, his play acting has gone on for too long, and he is now doomed to go on with it for the rest of his life. This is the core of George's problem. Having examined his "talent" he still does not know whether he possesses it or not. By the end of the

[24] *Op. cit.*, p. 51.

play we do not know whether George is in fact a true artist suffering from the normal momentary doubts common to most creative people, or whether he is an artificiality of the same type as Archie Rice. Osborne and Creighton seem reticent to pass judgement. What we do know is that George shrinks away from the pain of a fully imaginative existence, preferring to surrender his responsibility as an artist to the morphine of family life with the Elliots. He condemns himself to live with the euthanasia of the Elliots' love, despite his protests made to Ruth, which showed him to be a man of perception.

> GEORGE. I have a mind and feelings that are all fingertips. Josie's mind. She can hardly spell it. And her feelings— what about them? All thumbs, thumbs that are fat and squashy like bananas, in fact, and rather sickly.[25]

This image could well serve as a frontispiece for any play by Osborne for it expresses perfectly his purpose, which is to illustrate the despair and helplessness of a man of feeling, false artist that he may be, surrounded by the sickly banana-like caricatures which pass today for imaginative human beings.

Ruth refuses George the taste of the "Brown Windsor" of love, and he consoles himself by persuading Josie to go to his room, where he seduces her. As they climb the stairs they are watched by Percy, who remains rooted to the spot, a symbol of our inability to change anything in this life of acceptance. Once again the dramatic, if contrived, curtain.

The Third Act heralds the appearance of Barney Evans, theatrical producer of such masterpieces as *Slasher Girl* and *My Skin is My Enemy*. Evans persuades George to "tart-up" one of his plays in order to make it appeal to the public. George has been ill, and Ruth on her return from the doctor's to collect the result of the diagnosis tells the family that George has T.B. This tends to heighten out sympathy for him at a point when we begin to see him in a bad light. He eventually returns from hospital cured of the disease, only to find that Josie is pregnant, and worse, that Percy has discovered George is a married man. George becomes maudlin when he realises

[25] *Op. cit.*, p. 59.

Ruth is finally leaving and begs her not to go. Ironically one of George's plays has become successful, but Ruth still questions the nature of his existence, and as he recites his own epitaph, she leaves. George is left talking to himself:

> GEORGE. . . . . Even his sentimental Epitaph is probably a pastiche of someone or other, but he doesn't quite know who. And in the end, it doesn't really matter.[26]

This self-pitying speech depends on Ruth lacking any critical faculties and she, in fact, adds only comments to help the monologue along. When she finally leaves, he is left alone and heroic.

Adequately explaining away his marriage (the separated wife ironically being Percy's favourite television star), George settles for marriage with Josie. The play ends with George protesting once again at "those bloody birds", but mechanically he accepts his future with the words, "Come on, Mum, let's dance". "It doesn't really matter" sums up George's life, his glimpse of something better has been stifled and shut away. No longer can he shake his fist at the photograph of Mrs Elliot's son, or call him a stupid-looking bastard as a warning to himself, for George has now become that person.

The final picture is frightening, and we can have little hope for George's happiness. It is interesting to reflect that at the end of each of the three plays discussed so far, the prospects for the central character are disturbingly bleak. George Dillon becomes most pitiable, and most human, at that moment when he accepts that his future is to dance with Mum into eternity—he has become part of "the great society". The inevitability of this existence is truly tragic. We are not dealing with a "has been", reduced in circumstances, but with a "hasn't been", something much more pathetic.

IV

In *Luther*, his next play, Osborne tried to balance the idea of man as an individual with that of man as part of society,

---

[26] *Op. cit*, p. 87.

and the play communicates a sense of real importance. The audience were able to feel that Martin Luther was a man of significance, and that the events dealt with were of some moment. The historical material is presented in a straightforward fashion, with Martin's own speeches used wherever possible. Thus the play relies on documentary sources for much of its action and dialogue. In the balance between man as an individual and man in society the emphasis in the play is strongly on the former and we witness the development of Martin's physical obsession, his constant self-condemnation, and the unsatisfactory nature of his filial relationship. We should remember that in real life he was a man full of contradictions, and in whom many paradoxical features were combined.

Luther is in essence a narrative, and Osborne is at his weakest as a story-teller, for his true art lies in his feeling for "instinctive theatre" rather than prepared situations. Consequently, Osborne makes the play resemble a medieval historical pageant, full of vivid theatrical moments, such as the Pope's hunting scene, Tetzel's indulgence speech, or Martin's soliloquy at the Diet of Worms. Some thread of narrative is provided, however inaccurate, as we follow Martin through his battle with his own sense of guilt, towards a more personal relationship with God, resting on the basis of simple faith. The subject was an obvious one for Osborne, for he shares with Luther the same search for identity, and the same refutation of the inherited traditions of life. Martin is symbolic of Osborne's "grand design", the recovery of a personal belief and a private conscience. The fact that the monk is uncertain of the way in which to reform the world may well be another parallel with Osborne. Obviously the playwright intended *Luther* to have more than purely historical interest:

> It's difficult to pin-point just how *Luther* started. It's been brewing over a long period. I wanted to write a play about religious experience and various other things, and this happened to be the vehicle for it. Historical plays are usually anathema to me, but this isn't a costume drama. I hope that it won't make any difference if you don't know anything about Luther himself, and I suspect that most people don't. In fact the

historical character is almost incidental. The method is Shakespeare's or almost anyone else's you can think of.[27]

The play has an overall theme, a man's rebellion against the world he was born into, and his attempt to understand life through a personal relationship with God. As such, *Luther* may be regarded as of more than strictly historical or theological appeal. Dante's words, "In the middle of the journey of life, I came to myself in a dark wood where the straight way was lost" apply no less forcibly to Martin Luther than they do to Jimmy Porter. The hero of *Look Back In Anger* retreats into a world of bears and squirrels, whilst Martin seeks salvation in the arms of his nun and their son's love. Osborne's statements in the play, like those of Luther, are about general human behaviour and they have universal and timeless validity. Indeed one of the drawbacks to the play is the alternation between "ancient "and "modern", especially as far as speech is concerned.

Once again Osborne embraced certain Brechtian alienation techniques in this production. The back-cloth, a minimal gaunt tree, allows us to see Martin from the outside, a position which is further supported by the use of an interlocutor who announces time and place for each scene. The whole emphasis on fleshly torment is Brechtian in its very nature, and whilst we can clearly see the individual rebel, we are not entirely convinced about the religious reformer. Have we seen an indomitable conscience battling with the consecrated rottenness of the established Church? Probably not, if we consider religion as an entirely intellectual attitude: but if we hold that it should take account of all human suffering, mental and physical, then Martin's "pain in the bowels" is at once significant and symbolic. As to what to make of this monk, Osborne has left room for the audience's perception. Above all he has allowed one to determine for oneself what Martin perceived as the meaning of justification by faith rather than by works, and this is the very crux of the play.

Luther is a coarse, gross man, with a burning inner violence

---

[27] "That Awful Museum", John Osborne interview with R. Findlater. *Twentieth Century*, February 1961.

and indignation, perpetually demanding. He is capable of that feeling and capacity for suffering common to all Osborne "heroes". We soon see his panic and his despair when he pleads about his fear of the darkness and "the hole in it". From this despair stems the anger and rudeness of a man dissatisfied with the conventions of his day, yet not knowing what to do to change them. This helplessness finds its outlet in Martin's words for when an evil is to be damned he turns a flood of surging rhetoric against it. When he exposes the pitiful meaningless of the sacred relics, he condemns the peasants with the words:

> MARTIN. Your emptiness will be frothing over at the sight of a strand of Jesus beard, at one of the nails driven into His hands, and at the remains of the loaf at the Last Supper. Shells for shells, empty things for empty men. There are some who complain of these things, but they write in Latin for Scholars. Who'll speak out in rough German? Someone's got to bell the cat![28]

His humility here, in fact, is arrogance, another paradox in the make-up of the poor German monk! What indeed are we to make of his final betrayal of the peasants, when having incited them to revolt, he sides with the forces of law and order?

Martin is a man of flesh and a man of vision inextricably entangled, a portrayal we see erupting expressionistically throughout the play, first pained and bitter, finally arrogant and confident. A man as coarse and fleshy as he is learned and idealistic. The "beginning" of the play, devoted to the development of Luther's neuroses, is very theatrical. It concentrates on atmosphere, and on one dramatic image, the almost naked Martin prostrating himself before the cross on his acceptance into the Church. The remainder of the act explores the nature of Martin's relationship with his father, his physical trials, especially his painful constipation, and his mental problems concerning the basis of religious belief. The growing isolation of Martin in the monastery is well depicted. His internal conflicts build pressures which in their outward

---

[28] *L.*, p. 62.

expression cut him off from his fellows. Much of the material for this act comes from Erik Erikson's psycho-analytical interpretation, *Young Man Luther*. Martin is shown to be so sensitive to religious ritual that he must either be ridiculing it or supernaturally inspired. His own confessions stand out starkly from the trivial concerns of the other monks:

> MARTIN. I am a worm and no man, a byword and a laughing stock. Crush out the worminess in me, stamp on me.
> BROTHER. I confess I have three times made mistakes in the Oratory, in psalm singing and Antiphon.[29]

His isolation is certainly more real than his commitment to God. The first scene ends dramatically when Martin throws a frightening epileptic fit at the realisation of God's task for him, unable to speak, jerking frenetically, he manages to gasp out his protest at being selected for special victimisation.

An equally vivid visual image confronts us at the beginning of the second scene, when Martin's anguish is symbolically represented by the figure of a man draped across the gleaming cutting edge of a gigantic butcher's knife. Martin is tormented by the dread of performing his first public Mass, yet with help he manages to perform it adequately. While he recovers from the emotional strain of the Mass, his father Hans, and a friend Lucas, sit drinking in the convent refectory.

When Luther eventually appears his father talks of his own worry that Martin was going to "fluff" the delivery of the Mass, and we realise that Martin is already beginning to question the nature of belief. Martin's filial relations become strained when his father rebukes him for having decided to become a monk instead of a magistrate or Burgermeister, or anything else he might have wished. Hans tells his son that a father deserves more than Martin has given him. Scornfully Martin answers:

> MARTIN. I've given you! I don't have to give you! I *am*— that's all I need give you. . . . All you want is me to justify *you*. Well I can't, and what's more I won't. I can't even justify myself.[30]

[29] *Op. cit.*, p. 19.   [30] *Op. cit.*, p. 41.

This scene is intensely personal as father and son explore their relationship, and though each in his own way admits his love for the other, they acknowledge at the same time their estrangement. We see in this how Martin will have the same emotions towards God, his need for love and his fear of rejection.

If Act One can be regarded as a psychological interpretation of the private world of Martin Luther, then the second act envelops the public world, giving a splashy chronicle of the period. In the first scene there is a savage parody of the selling of indulgences by Church officials. These "papers" enable believers to buy forgiveness for their sins, even those not yet committed! An indulgence ensures immediate entry into heaven dispensing with the need for purgatory. Osborne's caricature of Tetzel, the indulgence peddler, is theatrically quite devastating. It is so well constructed that the following scenes seem to be anticlimatic: yet we do, in fact, get the most detailed explanation of the nature of Martin's rebellion in them, an important ingredient, for one of the weaknesses of the play, is that we learn little of the inner compulsion which drove Martin to his final rejection of ecclesiastical doctrine. If anything, the effect of these scenes is to make us think that the Reformation stemmed from the single issue of indulgences.

In Scene Two, Luther is talking in the cloisters of the Eremite Monastery in Wittenberg, to the Vicar General of the Augustinian Order, Johan Von Staupitz, a quiet contemplative man. Staupitz tells Luther that his fanatical adherence to the rules of his order are only serving to make that authority seem ridiculous. The Vicar General fully realises that Martin is determined to supersede that authority and tries to placate him by sympathy, then in turn, by ridicule. He suggests that normal adherence to the Rule might give Luther the security he is seeking, but the young monk cannot be consoled, and asks Staupitz whether he ever feels humiliated to belong to a world that is dying. Martin's despair for humanity is expressed as he continues:

> MARTIN. . . . this must be the last age we're living in. There can't be any more left but the black bottom of the bucket.[31]

[31] *Op. cit.*, p. 54.

Staupitz, knowing that Martin will never be content to be a
spectator, tries to alleviate this despair by introducing the
subject of the young man's violent speeches against the practice
of indulgences, at the same time he reminds Martin of causes
still worth fighting for, yet reprimands him for the embarrass-
ment he causes by these attacks. Luther remains adamant,
logically pointing out the impossibility of the fact that eighteen
of Christ's Apostles are buried in Germany, when there were
originally only twelve! Staupitz gives Martin a final warning
to remember that he began his battle in the name of Jesus
Christ, and to do only as God commands. Luther's reply
again hints at the future:

> MARTIN. I will. Who knows? If I break wind in Witten-
> berg, they might smell it in Rome.[32]

Martin is eventually summoned before Cardinal Cajetan, the
Dominican General, and Rome's highest representative in
Germany. The Cardinal is smoothly cunning, and refuses to
be drawn into discussion with Martin, trying to gloss over the
troubles the Augustinian scholar has caused. Realising that
he cannot placate or persuade Martin to retract, he tells the
monk that he rejects his ideas on the grounds of their final
effect, scornfully rebuking Martin:

> CAJETAN. Oh, it's fine for someone like you to criticise and
> start tearing down Christendom, but tell me this: just tell
> me this: what will you build in its place?[33]

Martin's reply, that a withered arm is best amputated, causes
Cajetan to taunt Martin with his own personal doubts and he
shrewdly touches the nerve centre of Martin's fears about
belief. Finally the Cardinal demands that the young monk
retract lest he destroy the unity of the world. Martin, unable
to do so, asks that the matter be referred to the Pope.

The next scene, a pageant-like caricature, is set in the
hunting lodge of the Pope, Leo X. Leo enters, dressed in
expensive hunting clothes. He is a lively intelligent man, yet
indolent and restless. Impatient at being disturbed by the
arrival of Martin's letter, he listens as it is read. He realises

---

[32] *Op. cit.*, p. 60.   [33] *Op. cit.*, p. 72.

that this Teutonic "peasant" whom he calls a "double-faced German bastard" could well upset his elegant world, and the control of his own sophisticated Latins over the Christian hegemony. The Pope instructs that a letter be despatched to Cajetan to tell him to take Luther into custody, and that if the monk should not beg forgiveness, to banish and excommunicate him.

> POPE. There's a wild pig in our vineyard, and it must be hunted down and shot.[34]

This is an effective theatrical scene, with the decadence of the Church symbolised in the person of the foppish Pope, but it tells us little of the theological argument which raged at the time. In fact we never learn what makes Luther tick, intellectually or spiritually. This scene is a good example of one of the inherent weaknesses of the play. Brilliant in itself, it adds little to the whole, and these episodes gather no momentum. We might do well to remember, however, that debate, if it is to be effective, has to be lengthy and rather abstract, and as such, is not suitable for drama. Osborne has aimed at something other than an extensive exploration of the theological thought that went to make up the Reformation—he has tried to make the man "Luther" come alive.

The play affords many examples of Osborne's effective technique for ending acts with visually dramatic moments. Act Two ends with a scene in which the monks throw books of Canon Law and Papal Decretals into the huge fire outside the Elster Gate, Wittenberg. Martin furiously declaims the papal bull which excommunicates him and casts it into the flames. Falling to his knees he begs God to help him against the reason and wisdom of the world, he prays on as the red glow of the flames envelop him.

At the Diet of Worms, April 1521, Martin defends the heresy of his writings before the assembly. Using the Scriptures as defence, he demands to be told what his lies are. Eyk, the Chancellor of Ingolstadt, in disputation with Martin, asks the monk to retract his books and their errors, and not cast doubt on the holy orthodox faith which had been established by "the

---

[34] *Op. cit.*, p. 78.

most perfect legislator known to us, a faith defined by sacred councils, and confirmed by the Church". Martin's answer serves to condemn him further:

> MARTIN. . . .—I don't believe in Popes or councils—unless I am refuted by Scripture and my conscience is captured by God's own word, I cannot and will not recant, since to act against one's conscience is neither safe nor honest. Here I stand; God help me; I can do no more. Amen.[35]

In these words lies the crux of Luther's problem, and of all men who seek to satisfy their own conscience rather than satisfy the rules. Newman later made the same point when he stated, "I shall drink to the Pope, if you please, but to my conscience first, and the Pope afterwards".

The narrative then jumps four years to 1525 and the Peasants' Revolt, represented off-stage by the sound of cannon, marching songs, and the cries of wounded men. The story of the uprising is related by the Knight, a symbolic figure, whose long monologue almost obscures the fact that Osborne has avoided the issue of stating Martin's position concerning the peasants' movement. To have embroiled Luther in the revolt would be to make him a political innovator, as well as a theological one, and although Martin sought to remodel the Church, he did try to find security via faith, and because of this, may well have not thought it worthwhile to cause greater chaos by supporting the peasants. The Knight is no more a capable adversary to Luther than Tetzel, Staupitz, or Cajetan. The peasant monk is never in danger throughout the play, and even though the Knight harangues Martin, his words are too exhausted to be threatening, his only telling statement, apart from some shrieking hyperbole, is to tell Luther:

> KNIGHT. . . . you're a poet, but do you know what most men believe in, in their own hearts—because they don't see in images like you do—they believe in their hearts that Christ was a man like we are, and that He was a prophet and a teacher, and they also believe in their hearts that His supper is a plain meal like their own—if they're lucky enough to get

[35] *Op. cit.*, p. 85.

it—a plain meal of bread and wine! A plain meal with no
garnish and no word. And *you* helped them to believe it![36]

Martin, provoked by this, roars in pain at the God whom he
expected to keep His Word. When the Knight finally leaves he
curses Martin to stew with his nun—a plea which is realised in
the diminutive final scene of the play. The end of the play
is quite inconclusive, for while all was once certain to Martin,
now nothing is. He is complacent, married to his nun Katherine,
and unashamedly nostalgic. With his infant son cradled in his
arms, he murmurs:

> MARTIN. You should have seen me at Worms. I was almost
> like you that day, as if I'd learned to play again, to play out
> on the world like a naked child. "I have come to set a man
> against his father" I said, and they listened to me. Just
> like a child. Sh! We must go to bed, mustn't we? A
> little while, and you *shall* see me. Christ said that, my son.
> I hope that'll be the way of it again. I hope so. Let's
> just hope so, eh? Let's just hope so.[37]

Here Osborne seems to be interested in providing the same
kind of hopeful anchorage point, with which to end the play,
as he found for *Look Back in Anger*. Yet even in such a personal
scene, a reference to Worms is made, and this fault can be
found throughout the play—for whilst the themes are worked
out in a personal way, they are all adapted to the same historical
colouring, and this weakens them by splitting the play, as we
said earlier, into ancient and modern.

The play ranged between two points, from the serenity of
life in the monastery at the beginning, to the final peace of
married life within the same cloisters, twenty-one years later.
The panorama has stretched over these years and of necessity
has been a series of *tableaux*—an expansion of life between two
contracted points. While we may fault *Luther* on the grounds
of its inconsistency, or its lack of profound thought; its aim is
to be a dramatic portrait of a human being who had a great
effect upon the Christian world. A man in fact who split this
world in two. Perhaps too much has been included and some
ideas fall flat because there is not sufficient time to develop

[36] *Op. cit.*, p. 90.   [37] *Op. cit.*, p. 102.

them, but it cannot be easy, when using realistic methods, to
show on stage a man wrestling more with his own conscience
than with personal enemies. Neither can we criticise the playwright for leaning too heavily on borrowed sources, for he has
himself admitted that the play is meant to be half chronicle,
half interpretation. The technique is that of all Osborne plays,
independent monologues are cut into one another and pass for
dialogue; once again there is no protagonist worthy of the
name opposed to the hero. The charge that the flesh plays
too important a part compared to the "spirit" is in fact easily
refuted. Martin's physical pains are at once a symbolic expression of his mental battle, and an effort by Osborne to give
human appearance to a figure who in the minds of most people
today is a dusty theological "object" of the past. To show
Martin's constipation, his indigestion, his excessive perspiration,
is to show him as an ordinary human being. A man who would
appeal to the earthy German peasantry, and who would be able
to incite them to action. He is a direct contrast to the effeminate,
sophisticated Latin churchmen of the period, surely a fact which
helped Martin, as Staupitz states, to achieve important ends:

> STAUPITZ. You've taken Christ away from the low mumblings
> and soft voices and jewelled gowns and the tiaras and put
> Him back where He belongs. In each man's soul. We owe
> so much to you.[38]

Some argue that the play does not contain anything to sub-
stantiate Staupitz' view, and that Osborne's Martin lacks the
personality to achieve what the historical Luther did. But
cannot ordinary flesh be remarkable, can great men not have
earthly pains? Surely by seeing Martin's personal problems
and anguishes we know more of him and his motives than we
would from a detailed exposition of his intellectual powers.
The monk is meant to come alive—no amount of intensive
theological argument would necessarily achieve this more
effectively than Osborne's glossy characterisation. The playwright pursues his narrow theme quite relentlessly. The
theme gives no analysis of the causes of the Reformation, it
rather concentrates on the rebellion of one man against the

[38] *Op. cit.*, p. 100.

accepted belief and habit of the world into which he was born. It is an attempt to secure a personal understanding of what "conscience" and "faith in God" mean. Hence the personal and private peace allowed Luther at the end of the play.

The most objective argument against the play, is that too much of the action is reported. We are never able to see Martin at the point of focus, as it were. The treatment of the Peasants' Revolt leaves us rather in the air about Martin's part in the uprising, except that he sided with the forces of law and order. Osborne includes too much in his general attack, and this tends to detract from the central theme of Martin's awakening conscience. Some things are over-stressed, for example the same point regarding the idolatry and iconoclasm of the Established Church is made in successive scenes with Tetzel, Cajetan, and Pope Leo. The reason for Martin's ambivalent attitude towards authority is hinted by Osborne to have stemmed from the nature of his relationship with his father: but, having suggested this, the playwright does nothing more to clarify the picture. Finally those ideas of Luther's we do see developed, such as the sale of indulgences, are expanded at a rather simple intellectual level. Luther's real problem— the nature of faith—is hardly ever discussed, and surely the Reformation was essentially an intellectual movement, though we might do well to remember the play was called *Luther* and not *The Reformation*.

V

In *Inadmissible Evidence* Bill Maitland, the "hero", tries desperately to contact people already out of reach, and his voice surges on in endless repetition. The play is a protest at things which cannot be helped. Maitland is on trial, asking to be judged, yet self-judging at the same time. He accepts culpability, but protests at the severity of the sentence. Nicol Williamson who played the taxing role of Bill Maitland commented:

> This isn't a play about a man *going* down the drain. It's about a man *slipping* down the drain and desperately fighting not to do so.[39]

[39] *The Saturday Review*, 8 Jan. 1966.

G

The play begins in the middle of that decline, for we never know Maitland as a competent, complete man.　We see first the trial scene, something which more naturally would have been the epilogue of the play.　The vagueness of the nightmare trial becomes clearer as the play progresses, and the trial itself fore-shadows the action of the rest of the play.　It is superbly con-structed, its episodic form revealing Bill to us and to himself, as he slowly "slips down the drain".　The action of the play is the inadmissible evidence of the trial; Bill's self-destruction continues as the others leave him, and he is reduced to a tragic state beyond human dignity.　With such a complete moral disintegration Bill is left in the isolation of his own hell, with the knowledge he has nowhere to go.　Osborne breaks down the naturalistic progression of the story as the hero collapses.　We enter into his consciousness, and experience Bill's hysteria as he loses control and those around him withdraw.

As the trial scene begins, Bill stands downstage in the Dock, bemused and inert.　At the back of the stage on a high green bench sits the Judge, representing, symbolically, Bill's con-science.　The indictment of Bill's life is read to him, and his spluttered answers are a protest against those parts of modern society which deny the individual, thwart his emotions, and destroy his feeling.　Recognising the horror of the machine which is trampling him underfoot, Bill tries to protest, yet knows he is helpless.

> BILL.　. . . I never hoped or wished for anything more than
> to have the good fortune of friendship and the excitement and
> comfort of love and the love of women in particular.　I made
> a set at both of them in my own way.　With the first, with
> friendship, I hardly succeeded at all.　Not really.　No.　Not
> at all.　With the second, with love, I succeeded in inflicting,
> quite certainly inflicting, more pain than pleasure.　I am not
> equal to any of it.　But I can't escape it, I can't forget it.　And
> I can't begin again.　You see?[40]

This is the nature of Bill's despair.　Life is too much for him.　Where Jimmy Porter was frightened because he had little hope of the future, Bill is frightened because he has no real past.

[40] *I.E.*, p. 20.

We begin to sympathise with this fumbling solitary creature, but we must also appreciate the other side of his nature, for whilst he desires love and friendship, he can be quite venomous, as he readily admits:

> BILL. I myself am more packed with spite and twitching, with revenge than anyone I know of. I actually often, frequently, daily want to see people die for their errors. I wish to kill them myself. . . .[41]

It is between these two extremes that the excitement of the play is generated. We may feel pity for Bill, and compassion at his efforts to seek response, yet we know that with his spite and shallowness he is unworthy of love. The cause and effect are never made clear, nor is it really necessary that they should be.

As the nightmare scene ends, Bill struggles into conscious-ness and the setting merges into the naturalist daily life of Bill's chambers. The Judge is transformed into Hudson, his managing clerk, and the Clerk of the Court becomes Jones, the "Junior assistant". The rest of the act outlines the deteriorating situation of Maitland's practice and his personal relations. It contains many "cheap digs" at the masses, several sexual and topographical jokes, with which Osborne could be accused of playing to the gallery. There are some good examples of the playwright's vituperative social invective. At one point Bill describes his secretary's boy-friend as a ". . . tent peg. Made in England. To be knocked into the ground".[42] As usual Osborne wraps up much of the criticism in humour, nevertheless this is the "revolving gun turret" at large.

We witness Bill's inadequacy as the normal routine of the office proceeds, for whilst he criticises others he can cope with very little in life himself. His strained family relations are described, as is the need for the comfort of his mistress. Bill's irresponsible attitude is indicated by his cursory treatment of his secretary, Shirley, who is pregnant and about to leave the firm. Whilst not responsible for her condition, Bill has been her occasional lover, but thinks only of himself and his business when persuading her to stay. Maitland begins to realise his plight when he asks Hudson to become a partner. His managing

---

[41] *Op. cit.*, p. 108.   [42] *Op. cit.*, p. 27.

clerk hesitates, then admits that he too is thinking of leaving. Finally when Bill's first client of the morning, Mrs Garnsey, arrives, he is already defeated by the day and cannot cope with her and so bundles her out of his office.

The Second Act is more Osborne and less Maitland, and as such is less dynamic. There is little real point in enumerating the scenes of this play or their action, for they serve only as vehicles for the hero's progressive disintegration; they are alternatively filled with Maitland's vicious social criticism or his whimpering. Paradoxically, they seem full of wit and charity.

It is indeed difficult to know what to make of the central character. The concentration on Bill Maitland is so great that one might well question the need for Osborne to provide plots or supporting roles. Ironically, despite the venom directed against the mass mind it is still Bill who is crushed, the action of the play being both his defeat and his final protest.

Maitland's clients come and go, Mrs Garnsey, Mrs Tonks, Mrs Anderson (played by the same actress), all tell the same story and Bill slowly appreciates that he is listening to his own evidence. Maples, a homosexual client, forces Bill to accept that the two of them are alike in their compulsion to avoid the issue. This episode is deeply sympathetic and profoundly moving, but Osborne does revert to his older method of characterisation, and Maples is developed through long monologues. Bill, revealed to himself by Maples, tries desperately to impart a little of the wisdom he has gathered by experience to his daughter Jane. Yet even this is beyond him, for he is at first too sentimental and then finally too scornful of Jane's generation, its whims, and its values. His teenage daughter, by her impassive reception of his words, rejects Bill no less than the others. Her selfishness echoes his own. In this scene Bill becomes the mouthpiece for Osborne, as Jane becomes a representative of her generation. Even so, Bill's torrent of words show him at his most human and nostalgic moment. This monologue ends with Bill's final good-bye to his daughter for he knows she too has eluded him. Defeated in this task, tarnished by his inability to be impersonal or less righteous, he stands alone, betrayed by himself and by those he loves.

Eventually his mistress Liz comes to the office to tell him she too is leaving him and the play ends with Maitland phoning Anna, his wife, to tell her he won't come home but just stay in his office until somebody comes to get him.

Bill has exorcised himself. The love he demands is thwarted by his own inability to give love, an inability implied by his wide sexual appetite. In the span of the play we learn of his affairs with Shirley and Joy, his employees, and Liz, and there are numerous references to other liaisons. Yet all his women leave him, in much the same way that his wife and friends have turned their backs and disowned him. Bill is perpetually aware of the fate in store for him, but is defiantly certain that *his* values are correct rather than those of society. There is no paradox in this, for Bill thinks that society is indeed wrong. His downfall is that of a man trapped in the machine of progress, and as such it is representative of John Osborne's fundamental position. A position described by *Time* magazine:

> Osborne recoils at the world of the social contract symbolised by his lawyer-hero, the world of abstract concepts, impersonal institutions, dehumanised relationships, bounded in paper and ratified by the press. The sense of loss that permeates his plays is an unrequited yearning for the old blood ties of pre-industrial man, the organic community of honor and duty where man was knitted to man without intellectual sophistication or corporate complexity. The spectacle of a human worm turning on the office spit, the sapped vitality, the jangled nerves, the repetitive routines, all these are abrasively marshalled by Osborne to convey his vision of the modern world as a playing field of pain.[43]

Bill Maitland is the human worm on the hook, and *Inadmissible Evidence* an extraordinary monologue in which the defendant is also the witness. Tiring of his own voice, he condemns himself. Bill claims to have always kept things in their place, but we know that this, ironically, is exactly what he has been unable to do. His practice withers, taxis pass him by, his staff leave, and porters ignore him. Finally, his family and his mistress desert, and unable to fight on, Bill throws in the towel and admits the obscenity of his existence—the charge before the bench of his mind since the play began.

[43] *Time,* 10 Dec. 1965.

The play is the highest achievement to-date in Osborne's technique of the one-man play, for it is the first to categorically state that isolation is its theme. In it Osborne manages to fuse reasonably successfully, Bill's subjective vision of his decline with the more naturalistic elements in the play. As a hero Bill fits in better with the background. The other characters are not used for a specific purpose and then dropped, we get interaction and development. Shirley's need for revenge is greater than her need to stay at work and earn for the baby she's going to have; and Joy's awareness of Maitland's use of her body and her subsequent withdrawal strike exactly the right tone. Bill is unable to get emotional reassurance at any price, his attempt to buy Hudson with the offer of a partnership fails dismally.

The major weakness of the play is the reconciliation of Bill's insight into his failings, with the state of collapse he permits himself. This contradiction leads one to think that Osborne wanted to suggest that society is more at fault than the individual. The play can thus be interpreted as a compendium of the dangers of today. If this is so, then Osborne's dramatic achievement with *Inadmissible Evidence* is even greater, for he provides a continuously unfolding story of the decline and fall of an isolated human being.

The play's underlying theme is that there is no dream of perfection available to man. Where in society is there anything worthy of rousing us to significant action? Bill's state of mind reflects this attitude, for though he is desperately trying to escape the banality of it all, he is reduced to a state of hopeless despair: "I think I'll just stay here" are his last words. A man reduced to a final pathetic isolation. Life today is without precedent, and thus difficult to base on experience, which itself is unprecedented; what one needs is a moral order, and this is exactly what Bill Maitland lacks. The future has been taken out of his hands.

VI

A Patriot for Me is the most difficult of Osborne's plays to situate. It was commercially unsuccessful, but was stoutly defended by many influential critics. The McCarthy-Tynan disagreement is now legend. There is a solitary hero but not until the very end of the play is his true voice heard and we see him through other eyes than his own. Structurally the play is a series of short scenes showing the hero as he reacts to different circumstances.

It deals with events in the years 1890-1913 in the Austro-Hungarian Empire, ruled over by Franz-Josef and Elizabeth. Alfred Redl, the hero, is a low-born Jewish lieutenant in the Imperial Army, who rises to become Head of Intelligence; but because of his homosexuality, he is blackmailed into becoming a spy for Tzarist Russia. Owing to the open way in which the play discusses homosexuality it was not licensed for public performance. Miss Mary McCarthy discussing in *The Observer*, Osborne's motives for writing such a play, suggested that perhaps he wanted to show that homosexuals are security risks, or that anti-semitism was common in the Austro-Hungarian Army. She went on:

> Why did Osborne write this? What does he mean to say? Is it a free translation—or travesty—of the Profumo story? Or can it be an anti-militarist tract which boldly declares that if universal disarmament had been established in 1890 none of these Jews and homosexuals would have had to lead a life of trite glittering pretence, Dr Schoepfer would have been out of a job, or transferred to geriatrics, and as an additional bonus there would have been no World War I ?[44]

Continuing in this vein Miss McCarthy slated the characterisation, the dialogue, and Redl's dissimilarity to a true Osborne hero, concluding her remarks: "The chief merit of the enterprise was to give work to a large number of homosexual actors or perhaps to normal actors who could 'pass' for homosexuals". This last facetious remark expectedly brought forth the howl of protest it deserved, for it had no place in serious literary criticism. To be fair to Miss McCarthy she did make some cogent observations about Osborne's work in general, and her article was good newspaper copy, which was what it was supposed to be.

[44] *The Observer*, 4 Jul. 1965.

Should the play be interpreted as a denunciation of homosexuality? Or is it a defence of those who have the courage to be honest to themselves before they are honest to their country? Is it meant to be an attack on a social system, which, because of its hypocrisy, sacrificed an able servant? Perhaps Osborne was simply interested in homosexuality in the same way that Nabokov was in the love of pubescent girls? I think the best way to approach the play is to regard it as another "timeless" Osborne concept. If we emphasise the self-realisation and self-acceptance of Redl, then we may regard *A Patriot for Me* as part of Osborne's "public" voice. Redl gradually permits his desires and his true nature to emerge and determine the course of his life. He is perfectly aware that his deal with the Russians will eventually be discovered, but he is helpless to prevent the inevitability of this discovery. He accepts his fate knowing that society will not grant him happiness in any case. Redl is content to wait, as Maitland was, for someone to come. It would seem from the evidence of these two plays that Osborne was moving away from his view that the world can be changed, for the hopeful endings of *Look Back in Anger* and *Luther* give way to the abject acceptance of fate, to the Law Society and the loaded pistol of *Inadmissible Evidence* and *A Patriot for Me*. The committed socialist becomes less so.

The title of the play was suggested by a sentence of Emperor Franz III, who, when discussing the promotion of a junior officer remarked when told that the man was a patriot: "Ah! But is he a patriot for me?" It is a long and complex play, with twenty-three scenes, and a cast of ninety performers. The First Act concentrates on background, and the discovery by Redl of his repressed homosexuality—yet we see him first as an ambitious conformist. He is in fact very adaptable to people and situations. He involves himself as a second in an unsavoury duel, but is nevertheless promoted to Staff College, having made the appropriate tactful adjustments.

It is while celebrating this achievement at Anna's, a café-brothel, that he is disturbed "physically" by a good-looking young waiter, Albrecht, and later is singularly unsuccessful with a whore. An abrupt switch takes us to Warsaw, where Oblensky, head of the Russian Espionage network, is examining Redl's record to see if he is a possible recruit as a spy. Thus we see, side by side, the two elements of his downfall, his latent homosexuality and through this, his eminent suitability for blackmail.

Gradually Redl begins to admit to his nature. We see this in his relationship with the Countess, a "novelettish", beautiful Russian spy! He accepts her as a lover but can find little happiness with her, being unable to reciprocate her passion:

COUNTESS. Don't turn your head away.
REDL. Please!
COUNTESS. What is it? Me?
REDL. No. You're—you're easily the most beautiful . . . desirable woman I've ever. . . . There couldn't be. . . .
COUNTESS. It's not easy to believe.
REDL. Sophia: it's *me*. It's like a disease.[45]

Here we begin to witness Redl's struggle with his desire, but we get no explanation why a man who is apparently heterosexual at this stage of the play, becomes completely homosexual by the end of the play. We might also note that the dialogue, as we see it here, is much weaker than the normal "public" voice play, only very occasionally does the language rise to true Osborne stature.

Eventually Redl faces his conscience when his friend Taussig leaves him alone in a Viennese café, and a young man who has been watching him carefully, joins him in casual conversation. Redl asks him to go away, but the young man softly tells Redl: "I know what *you're* looking for". Redl rebukes him violently but we know that his fight with his own nature is almost over, and in the following scene we see him in bed with Paul, a young private. Redl asks the soldier why he won't keep the light on. Ironically, in his own affair with the Countess, Redl always insisted on turning out the light. The young man betrays Redl, opening the door to let in four of his friends who rob and beat up the officer. As Paul leaves he sarcastically tells Redl: "Don't be too upset, love. You'll get used to it."[46] Osborne has suggested Redl's homosexuality very deftly, and it is not until this moment that we have anything conclusive at all. His presentation of Redl is certainly restrained and greatly

[45] *P.M.*, p. 56.　　[46] *Op. cit.*, p. 69.

encourages the audience's sympathy. Redl is not a brave hero, and Osborne does not blame Redl's failings on society, by not doing so he increases our affection for Redl as a likeable character.

The highlight of the play is the "drag-ball" for which the playwright provides over three pages of detailed stage instructions and notes. The ball is sumptuously rendered, like a gilded bird cage in its colour and twittering. The participants are too numerous to mention individually but include the host, Baron Von Epp, dressed as Queen Alexandra, bejewelled dog collar, osprey feathers and all; and a Lady Godiva complete with gold lamé jockstrap. Redl, now some years older, is in his Colonel's uniform and is accompanied by his young lover, Lieutenant Stefan Kovacs. They are amused by, but wary of, the proceedings. The scene might have been taken straight from *The Merry Widow*, and as one character explains, the "drag-ball" is:

> BARON. . . . the celebration of the individual against the rest, the us's and the them's, the free and the constricted, the gay and the dreary, the lonely and the mob, the little Tzarina there and the Emperor Francis Joseph.[47]

The scene is spiced with a humour which is lacking from the rest of the play, which further heightens the gaiety of the ball and its contrast to the everyday life of the Empire.

If this scene, however unfunctional, is the most theatrical of the play, then that in which Oblensky, the head of Russian Intelligence confronts Redl with his life story, and "enlists" him to the Russian cause, is also very effective. Redl gets our sympathy, not so much for what he is, but for the plight he finds himself in. He has no answer to Oblensky who reminds him:

> OBLENSKY. Would you, do you think *could* you change your way of life, what else do you want after all these years, what would you do at your age, go back to base and become a waiter or a washer up, sit all alone in cafés again, constantly watching? What are you fit for?[48]

[47] *Op. cit.*, p. 77.   [48] *Op. cit.*, p. 96.

The affluence and success of the passing years has cushioned Redl against the harsh realities of life thus he accepts Oblensky's proposition, in doing so he tightens the noose around his neck, for the income derived from his spying activities serves to cut him off even further from reality.

Eventually Redl loses Stefan to the Countess, who is pregnant by the young man, and in a scene reminiscent of that between Ruth and George in *Epitaph for George Dillon*, the two sink their teeth into each other. When Redl taunts the Countess with her lack of knowledge of the true delights of Stefan's body, she bites back at him:

> COUNTESS. God. I'm weary of your self-righteousness and all your superior railing and your glib cant about friendship and the Army and the way you all roll out your little parade: Michelangelo and Socrates, and Alexander and Leonardo. God, you're like a guild of housewives pointing out Catherine the Great.[49]

Osborne is completely honest as far as homosexuality is concerned, allowing Redl to answer the charge against him:

> REDL. So, you'll turn Stefan into another portly middle-aged father—with—what did you say once—snotty little longings under their watch chains and glances at big, unruptured bottoms.[50]

This is one of the few examples of general social criticism which the play provides, though of course its central theme implies a rejection of the standards of a society which persecutes any isolated group to such an extent as it does homosexuals. The Countess would be a worthy opponent for any Osborne hero, but unfortunately Redl is not typical of them, being almost totally devoid of spunk until the end of the play. In fact these emotional outbursts by Redl, when Osborne reverts to monologue, are all the more surprising because we are not used to them, or such self-exposure. These vivid attacks are thrown in without any prior build up. When Redl rails out at Viktor, Stefan's replacement, we hear the familiar Osborne tones, in a speech which is very much parallel to that of Bill's against his

---

[49] *Op. cit.*, p. 101.   [50] *Op. cit.*, p. 102.

daughter Jane. Redl is furious at Viktor's ability to take but not give:

> REDL. You are thick, thick, a sponge, soaking up. No recall, no fear. You're a few blots. . . . All you are is young. There's no soft fat up here in the shoulder and belly and buttocks yet. But it will. Nobody loves an old, squeezed, wrinkled pip of a boy who was gay once. Least of all people like me or yourself. You'll be a vulgar fake, someone even toothless housewives in the market place can bait. . . . You little painted toy, you puppet, you poor duffer. . . .[51]

Redl no longer makes any pretence at conformity, he has become honest to himself. He acknowledges the pathetic fate awaiting the"us's". And we must admire Osborne for writing such speeches on a topic so many have avoided. Paradoxically, Redl is not so honest in admitting that he is a Jew, for he will own up to both his crime and his homosexuality before he will announce that he is Jewish.

The play quickens appreciably towards its end as Redl's fate becomes more and more obvious, and as he completes his process of self-discovery. His denunciation of the Spanish influence on the Empire, after he has signed his confession, is the point to which the whole play moves, for in it, Redl becomes truly himself:

> REDL. . . . I think I hate the Spaniards most of all. Perhaps that's the flaw . . . of my character. . . . Those damned Spaniards were the worst marriage bargain the Hapsburgs ever made. Inventing bridal lace to line coffins with. They really are the worst. They stink of death, I mean. It's in their clothes and their armpits, quite stained with it, and the worst is they're so proud of it, insufferably. Like people with stinking breath always puff and blow and bellow an inch away from your face. . . .[52]

This is his most articulate and dramatic speech, steeled by brandy and facing certain death, Redl bursts out in the characteristic scathing language of an Osborne hero.

Redl accepts the proffered pistol, and while his superiors wait in the dark street outside, he shoots himself. This scene would have provided an adequately contrived finale, but the

[51] *Op. cit.*, p. 118.   [52] *Op. cit.*, p. 122.

play in fact has some form of epilogue, for the closing scene depicts Oblensky once more in front of his projection screen, looking at the image of Dr Schoepfer, the Jewish neuropathologist whom the drag-ball guests had ridiculed for his inquiry into their "peculiarity". This provides a further note of mystery, for what does Osborne mean? Is Schoepfer the next candidate for blackmail? Is this the new girl at the ironing board? Or does Osborne mean to show that the use of Freudian theory by society in transferring responsibility for homosexuality to the individual leads to unpatriotic acts? Possibly Schoepfer might even represent another Jewish climber ready to betray the Empire? The first answer, that Schoepfer is no more than the next likely candidate for the Russian Secret Service seems the most likely. Had any other face been flashed on the screen we would have been equally bemused, and a similar number of interpretations could be offered, as they can for the Misha Lipschutz episode, which seems only there to give Osborne the opportunity to write some mad dialogue.

The play is certainly problematical—"art must have meaning"—seems to be a particular twentieth-century problem. Yet if we regard *A Patriot for Me* as a play about human beings in much the same way as we have considered Osborne's other works, then it becomes much more explicable. It establishes, through a particular case, that of Redl and his homosexuality, the tragic dilemma of society's inacceptance. The play is an extensive, rambling journey into the nature of a certain kind of human existence, demonstrating in passing, that the pressure of society can destroy that which it seeks to preserve. It does this, by forcing the sexual deviant to choose between being a patriot to his society or patriot to himself. If that particular man, or woman, is in a position of public responsibility then the choice is all the more dangerous and important. Alfred Redl chose to be a special kind of patriot, one who valued more than his love for his country, a desire to realise the personality he felt to be his honest self. If we all do the same who is to say the world would not be a better place? If we regard the play in this light, then we can see once again that Osborne is concerned with removing those things which prevent an individual, in this instance, a homosexual, from realising his full emotional expression. This is a timeless problem, and Redl may have some special significance for us today, for he succeeded in living a "whole" life in a dead Empire. His crime is that he ignored society and the State, devoting himself to himself.

VII

The central character of *Time Present* has remarkable affinities with Jimmy Porter, for Pamela too needs the same affection and respect that he lacked. Her recognition of this echoes Jimmy's forlorn pleas:

> PAMELA. Yes, I believe in friendship, I believe in love. Just because I don't know how to doesn't mean I don't. I don't or can't.[53]

Deprived of this friendship Pamela adopts Jimmy's answer, and her sardonic invective spits out throughout the play. The two plays have other similarities for in both the past seems much better that the time present, the Colonel and the Shakespearian actor live in the same world. Indeed, we could level the same criticism at the two works. Does the anger of the "heroes" result from their disgust at the insensitive amoral society of today, or does it grow from their frustration at not being able to live in the past—where they would "belong"?

Unlike *Look Back in Anger*, *Time Present* is a two-act play, but with the same lengthy "fill-in background" opening. We see Edith, Pamela's mother, and Pauline, her pretty young step-sister, sitting in the apartment she shares with Constance, an M.P. They are resting between visits to hospital, where Gideon Orme, Pamela's actor father lies dying. There are long expository passages about characters not yet met, and when Constance, who is in her early thirties, enters there is no break in this process. It is not until the arrival of Pamela herself some minutes later that the first sparks of Osborne's invective begin to fly, with the description of Pauline's waiting friend:

> PAMELA. I suppose that hippie outside belongs to you? Does he have a name or is he a group? It was a bit difficult to tell if he was one or several.[54]

---

[53] *T.P.*, p. 28.   [54] *Op. cit.*, p. 22.

Pamela continues to taunt her step-sister with jibes about psychedelic companies and her "ecstatic" ventures, and Osborne seems very well up in Chelsea vernacular.

When Edith and Pauline finally leave we see how exhausted Pamela is by her vigil at Orme's bedside, but she is not too tired to stop questioning herself:

> PAMELA. Oh I *am* selfish. I won't give money to take full page ads about Vietnam or organise them like Mama. I certainly wouldn't give money. I'm too mean. Too mean and too poor. Just because I share a bath and an inside lavatory doesn't mean I'm not poor. Well, does it? I'm even unemployed. Oh, you think it's funny, but I am, I'm unemployed.[55]

We might at this stage begin to believe that Pamela's disillusionment comes from the fact that she is a "resting" actress, but she follows these words with a rambling appraisal of her dying father and her love for him and for his beliefs immediately becomes clear. Once again Osborne's atavistic longing for a past order intrudes into the present. Of Orme, Pamela cannot speak or feel too highly, and his off-stage presence begins to become more alive and dominant than those on stage.

The minor characters are barely drawn throughout the play, they seem almost perfunctorily thrown in, and any character revelation is but slowly worked out, interspersed with Pamela's witty invective. Murray sums this up with his description of Pamela:

> MURRAY. You treat people as walk-on's.[56]

Words sadly applicable to all Osborne's heroes, and Pamela certainly has no opponents; if an opportunity existed surely it is with Constance, but it is not until the very end of the play that she begins to exist without Pamela. So Pamela talks on, heaping scorn on contemporary society. The targets of her attack include—politicians, critics, lady writers, dieting, sex, education, economics, other actresses, memorial services, sun-tan, high taxes, homosexuals—and even her own needs. She is virtually a non-stop monologue protesting at the banality

---

[55] *Op. cit.*, p. 28.   [56] *Op. cit.*, p. 64.

of life, too nervous to stop to think, she loses herself in a torrent of humorous cynicism:

> PAMELA. If you've got "A" levels, we're after you! And even
> if you've only got "O" levels, we're *still* interested. Fancy
> lower streams of the poor little devils, upper levels of the
> bigger fish. I'd be in no stream at all. All those school
> inspectors and examiners and seducers from industry hanging
> about like men in raincoats, offering prospects and excite-
> ment and increments. How awful. If a man comes up to
> you, darling, however friendly he might be, talking about
> your "A" levels, don't, repeat, don't talk to him. He's
> after *you*, he wants to make a University challenger out of
> you. Don't talk to them, they're sick. Yes, but Mummy's
> known it for a long time. Get back home before the park
> gates close or he'll take out his careers section in the *Daily
> Telegraph* and show it to you.[57]

This humour is curiously reminiscent of Jimmy Porter's threat that Cliff will end up in *The News of the World* for molesting a cabbage. Like Jimmy, Pamela drones on, but there is even less action in *Time Present* than in *Look Back in Anger*.

We get some slight progression in the plot when Murray, Constance's younger lover, comes to the flat: but Pamela seems quite uninterested in him, although Constance with some form of unconscious lesbianism thrusts him at her. She comes close to dismissing him out of hand with a sweeping generalisation, something she is very prone to:

> PAMELA. I think Murray is one of those intellectuals who
> thinks all actors live in a narrow, insubstantial world, cut
> off from the rest of you. Well, kid yourself not. You're all
> of you in Show-Business now. Everybody. Of course,
> Orme was never in Show-Business.[58]

Again Pamela's distinction between the present and the past is apparent, and as Osborne's mouthpiece she voices only too obviously the author's comment about contemporary values. An even more perfunctory entrance is afforded to Edward, a casual ex-lover of Pamela's: "one epic in two and half years, and a nose job". As Constance and Murray go off to the bed-room so Pamela and Edward talk about Orme; when they

---

[57] *Op. cit.*, p. 40.   [58] *Op. cit.*, p. 48.

are interrupted by the telephone, Pamela learns of her father's death. She blames herself for mistiming things, and we feel that she too one day may be left unloved, alone, to die.

We might note here the importance of telephone calls and letters or telegrams to the action of Osborne's plays. There are a host of examples: Alison's good-bye note, Archie's telegram, Bill's telephone calls, Pamela's news here, and K.L.'s suicide in *The Hotel in Amsterdam*. Plot development occurs outside the characterisation rather than within.

In Act Two we see that Pamela reacts to Orme's death by sleeping most of the day, and when awake, by drinking champagne. When her family appear at the flat some weeks later, she condemns them for having organised the memorial service for her father, from which they have just returned:

> PAMELA. Orme would have hated the idea. I don't think he ever went to a memorial service in his life. He'd have laughed his head off at the idea, rows of his friends having to listen to Handel and Wesley and knighted actors reading the lesson. He'd have thought it very common.[59]

Pamela leaves her mother in no doubt that she too thinks it petty and vulgar, and when her mother tries to turn the conversation into some kind of attack against Pamela herself, her solipsism becomes evident as she replies:

> PAMELA. I shall manage within my own, my own walls. I've no ambitions. I've told you: I love acting. I'm not so keen on rehearsals. I don't wish to be judged or categorised or watched. I don't want to be pronounced upon or do it for anyone.[60]

The action of the second half of the play revolves around the fact that Pamela has become pregnant by Murray. She decides on an abortion and phones Bernard, her homosexual agent, so that she may make arrangements. When Murray arrives he is unable to persuade her to think again and she shows him little warmth, in effect she pushes him back into Constance's arms:

> PAMELA. You will find each other. Or not. I don't want to talk about it. I won't be involved in your life or hers.

[59] *Op. cit.*, p. 54.   [60] *Op. cit.*, p. 59.

H

I'm sorry for both of you. Not much. A bit. You'll manage,
so shall we all. Just remember: what I should do now or at
any time is nothing to do with either of you. I owe you no
confidence.[61]

Pamela's withdrawal is almost complete. She seems quite
unmoved by her plight; in itself sex has never been an answer
to her problems, and this latest episode seems little more
troublesome than the rest.

A further irritation occurs when Abigail and Edward
descend upon the trio. Abigail has been greatly built up
throughout the play, for she is the star Pamela longs to be.
Having enjoyed yet another triumphal first night, at the end of
the celebrations, she cavorts ecstatically around the apartment
as Pamela watches exhaustedly. Unfortunately *Time Present*
came to a shuddering halt in the Royal Court production of
the play at this point, for Abigail lacked any kind of magic
whatsoever. It was literally impossible to believe that Pamela
could have got so worked up and spiteful over this girl:

> PAMELA.   . . . that great booby of a tinker bell, Abigail!
> Abigail: just because she's made a movie and someone's
> talked about the mystery behind her eyes, she's just myopic
> which enables her to be more self-absorbed than ever and
> look as if she's acting when she's just staring at wrinkles on
> your forehead.[62]

Having witnessed the theatrically-bred Pamela for the whole
of the play it was not possible to credit Abigail with the kind of
success she was supposed to have enjoyed, whilst Pamela sat
idly "resting" in the apartment. It seems probable that no
actress could overcome this weakness for Abigail is little more
than a sketchy stereotype. It is difficult to believe that this was
deliberate for surely Osborne was not intending to show us how
easily success is won. The play does not really recover from
this blow, and Osborne's stage morality seems at loggerheads
here too, for there is some heavy melodrama about the abortion,
yet the two women had no worries at all about "exchanging"
Murray.

[61] *Op. cit.*, p. 63.   [62] *Op. cit.*, p. 37.

Finally Bernard comes to collect Pamela, and as she leaves, Constance phones Murray as a reassurance to them all:

> CONSTANCE. . . . come on over . . . yes, now, please . . . I love you . . . I ache for you . . . Do you? Thank heaven for that . . . Darling . . . oh, my darling . . . Pamela's going to give me a lesson . . . yes, right . . . Don't be long. . . .[63]

Pamela has certainly tried to give us a lesson, and it is silly to pretend that Pamela is anything *much* more than a female Jimmy Porter. Life is passing her by, and like all of Osborne's heroes, she is unable to do anything, but watch helplessly from the sidelines. She is appalled at the hypocrisy and emptiness of contemporary life. Like Bill Maitland she tries to inspire love, but seems incapable of giving it. She is too human to live alone, but she cannot refrain from picking holes in those around her, and so *Time Present* moves from one bitchy monologue to another. Its weakness, as usual, is that there is little action and no worthy opponents for the central character. None of the walk-on parts match Pamela in their reality. When Abigail appears she does not exist in comparison with Pamela. There is no real progression in the play. From beginning to end there is little development of any consequence. There are no answers, there are precious few *new* questions. But there is Pamela herself, a finely drawn, fully-rounded character, sufficiently egoistic to be capable of challenging the well of emotional loneliness, and spitefully honest enough to mark anyone or anything which stands in her way.

VIII

It would be incorrect to suggest that Osborne breaks new ground in his latest play by taking a group as his subject, for we hear only one voice, that of Laurie, who assumes full control of the other characters at the very beginning of the play. The rest of the group remain tactful listeners. In the same way we gain nothing by extending the comparison between this play and Noel Coward's *Design for Living*, for *The Hotel in Amsterdam* is hardly a comedy and in it Osborne

[63] *Op. cit.*, p. 81.

plays down show-business loyalty, making his play sourly disenchanting when compared with Coward's.

Three show-business couples have escaped from the domination of their film mogul employer, K.L., to spend a long week-end of freedom in Amsterdam. They are amazed at their liberty and cannot help congratulating themselves on their bravado:

> LAURIE. ... we are relieved, unburdened, we've managed to slough off that monster for a few days. We have escaped, we deserve it, after all this time. Just to be somewhere he doesn't know where any of us are. Can't get near us, call us, ring us, come round, write. Nothing. Nix. For a few blessed days. No K.L. in our lives. [64]

They pretend to seek no more than this, yet we soon realise that this lull in their lives has more importance than they are willing to acknowledge. The three couples are successful, comfortably-off and fortyish, yet there is an air of disillusionment about them, the future no longer seems quite so inviting. Laurie, K.L.'s scriptwriter, is their leader, a talented effeminate man, who manages to get everybody else to do his dirty jobs. His wife Margaret is pregnant, but this brings little joy to either of them, and she is resigned to her life as it exists. Gus is the Cliff of the party, a film cutter, good natured and un-suspecting, his wife Annie is immensely more perceptive and intelligent. K.L.'s secretary, the ever-efficient Amy, and her painter husband Dan, complete the group.

They gloat over their escape throughout the first half of the play, happy in the thought that K.L. will never think of looking for them in Amsterdam. In their constant irreverence we begin to see signs of their own need for reassurance. They appear as naughty schoolchildren who seek a pat on the head and a consoling word.

The play has literally no action, yet one is gripped by the tension which exists, for the characters hardly dare to believe that they have in fact arrived, and that they are, at least for the time present, free and on their own. The moods of the play are determined by Laurie. The opening perfectly catches the

[64] *H.A.*, p. 93.

group's nervous hilarity at arriving abroad, independent of
K.L. It is almost as if they were afraid that Amy could not
efficiently arrange this trip without K.L.'s seal of approval.
Gradually as they relax and take their first drinks, Laurie
becomes more expansive, and with great *panache* he begins to
air his pet hates: air hostesses, the pill, effeminacy, marriage,
boredom, and worst of all begging relatives:

> LAURIE. I suppose you think her face is pitted by the cares
> of the working class life and bringing up sons on National
> Assistance. Well, it isn't. She has that face there because
> there's a mean grudging, grasping nature behind it.[65]

Through Laurie, Osborne manages to locate his usual mixed
bag of targets.

So they drink on, listening to Laurie; discussing which
rooms to occupy; where to eat. Even these elementary
decisions seem difficult. Several drinks later Laurie has
warmed to his task, and his compulsive bitchiness, in itself some
form of defence, gradually takes on more serious overtones as
he begins to question the group's ethics. Can they continue
to make up their own values as they go along?

> LAURIE. But what goods? I ask myself: can anything
> manufactured out of this chaos and rapacious timidity and
> scolding carry-on really *be* the goods. . . . Won't the goods
> be shown up by the way of the manner of their manufacture?[66]

As Laurie's mood changes so does the atmosphere of the play;
and reinforcing its air of empty suffocating inertia are his more
emotional pleas for affection, which slip out unaware from
amidst his general condemnation of the "Golden Sanitary
Towel Award" society:

> LAURIE. Working on your own. I could never live on my
> own. Oh, I have done. It's been all right for a time. But
> what about now and then, the steep drop and no one there.
> And no one to phone or too far away.[67]

Here, Laurie anticipates Bill Maitland's problem. Laurie fears
desperately that people will slip away and he tries to tighten
the ties of friendship around himself. Osborne is more

[65] *Op. cit.*, p. 91.   [66] *Op. cit.*, p. 108.   [67] *Op. cit.*, p. 104.

concerned with friendship and goodness in *The Hotel in Amsterdam* than in any of his other plays. Where before it has lain below the surface, in this play his plea for human warmth and sincerity is plainly expressed.

The curtain of the first act emphasises this plea, for, having acknowledged to Annie his fear of living or being left alone:

> LAURIE. I have sometimes. It can be all right for weeks on
> end even. But then. You have to crawl out of the well.
> Just a circle of light and your own voice and your own
> effort. . . .[68]

Laurie sits looking out across the stage, his eyes filled with terror at his future, as the lights slowly dim around him.

Act Two is more compact and has more action than Act One. Two evenings after their arrival the group sit around in the suite sipping their "first drink of the evening". They are much more relaxed, and are even enthusiastic about their visits and experiences. Once again they cannot decide where to eat, but now it seems less important. Laurie is noticeably less exhibitionist, and his self-defence is not so apparent. He is concerned with the collective happiness of the venture, and rambles on enthusiastically about the group sharing an old Victorian house in London when they return, hoping to establish an Owenite "New Harmony". Tiring of this idea because of the others' lack of enthusiasm he launches himself into a bitter attack on his greedy grasping relatives. Suddenly he halts in midstream to suggest that he is "the most boring man anybody has ever met".

As Dan and Laurie slowly get drunk, our sense of anticipation quickens for we feel something is bound to happen. Nothing has so far for the group, having escaped, have nothing important to do. Laurie cannot be spiteful to Margaret or any of the others for they are not the causes of his disquiet, and so we wait for some significant action. There is a knock at the door of the suite, and when Gus opens it, Gillian, Margaret's thirty-year-old sister stands there—a shocking reminder of London. Laurie is outraged for he has already reprimanded his wife for telling her sister where they have all gone for the

[68] *Op. cit.*, p. 119.

weekend. His attacks on Gillian bring him closer to Jimmy Porter's rhetoric than anything else in the play, and when Margeret confidingly ushers her sister away to find out why she has come, Laurie bursts out:

> LAURIE. ... I tell you, she's not going to blight our weekend. We've had ourselves something we want to have and we made it work and she's not going to walk in here on the last night and turn it all into a Golden Sanitary Towel Award Presentation.[69]

He rants on about Gillian and her turning the weekend into Agony Junction, but his sensitivity scents out her tightly stretched tension, for later when she returns with Margaret, and talks on compulsively about trivialities, Laurie bitterly interrupts her with the words "Gillian, for Christ's sake burst into tears ...". She does. It is a moment of great poignancy.

Another follows almost immediately, when, as the others slowly drift away to their rooms, Laurie and Annie are left alone. Laurie declares his affection for Annie with a delicacy so far lacking in his character. He chooses carefully a whole string of adjectives, and slowly, deliberately, putting them together makes poetry of his love for her:

> LAURIE. ... to me ... you have always been the most dashing ... romantic ... friendly ... playful ... loving ... impetuous ... larky ... fearful ... detached ... constant ... woman I have ever met ... and I love you ... I don't know how else one says it ... one shouldn't ... and I've always thought you felt ... perhaps ... the same about me.[70]

Hesitantly he asks for her love in return, not daring to open himself further. Annie responds, yet both know there is little hope for their love to blossom fruitfully. It must remain stifled and withheld, even though it is obvious that Laurie's own marriage is dwindling into nothing.

Osborne has managed his tempo well in Act Two, for we see the relaxed group abruptly woken by Gillian's arrival, the gentle declaration of illicit love between Laurie and Annie, and finally, in a short sharp twist, the discovery by phone that K.L. has committed suicide. The God needed the worshippers

[69] *Op. cit.*, p. 132.   [70] *Op. cit.*, p. 139.

more than they needed a deity. They worship because they have wanted to worship. They are on their knees through choice. So the action we have anticipated throughout the play finally occurs, yet we are unmoved by it. So heavy is the air of fatality and emptiness that we can only imagine the group reliving the pattern elsewhere. Through their lack of ability to make choices and adjustments, and primarily through their want of the right kind of effort, they are left stranded, ever damned, with little past and no future.

The Hotel in Amsterdam is not a play about show-business, or even show-business people, although it does give us some telling insight into the fears and anxieties of creative people. The play emphasises the artist's need for encouragement and we see this only too clearly in Laurie. When he tires his friends with his "gimmick" Italian he quickly drops it, and turns elsewhere to earn their applause. At the same time Laurie symbolises the creative artist's pain and disillusionment, his angry frustration, and his disenchantment, even with money and success:

> LAURIE. . . . I'm certainly not spoiled. I work my drawers
> off and get written off twice a year as not fulfilling my early
> promise by some philistine squirt drumming up copy, some-
> one who's got as much idea of the creative process as Dan's
> mother and mine rolled into one lazy minded lump of misery
> who ever battened off the honest efforts of others.[71]

Osborne's position on this subject has always been candidly expressed, but never more so than in these words of Laurie's.

The play is certainly about friendship and the nature of love. Both Laurie's happiness to be with his friends, and his affectionate thankfulness for Annie's love stress this aspect. The six are all essentially good people, bewildered that, given what they have, they are not satisfied or even superficially happy. Laurie's genuine pleasure with his friends permits us to see him at his most disarming, and as we did with Jimmy Porter, we can forgive some of his unpleasant remarks about the supposedly less fortunate.

The Hotel in Amsterdam is a damning moral document, a

[71] *Op. cit.*, p. 99.

finely observed commentary on the state of affairs in the society we inhabit. As such, its honesty and truthfulness are invaluable. Laurie searches not only for himself, he searches for us. Can K.L. or God only be put off by love?

The play is never trite nor facile even though the style permits the playwright to throw in as many sarcasms as he wishes, and the pungent disturbing voice of the hero demands our response. We can only sympathise with the gradual tightening of the circle of friendship of the creative "us's" as they exclude the world beyond. At the same time it is an admission of their waning energy, and their inability to do anything which might decisively alter their lives. Like Maitland they can only sit and wait.

VI

The Private Voice

SATIRE needs to be objective, and while Osborne's plays contain much social criticism it is rarely logical or even accurately directed, the character who utters the rebuke being more important than the object under attack. In other words Osborne's social standpoint is subjective, and he is thus unsuited to write satire.

I

The World of Paul Slickey, first performed at the Pavilion Theatre, Bournemouth, on 14 Apr. 1959, was an attempt at musical satire. David Pelham, who presented the play, wrote in the hand-out blurb: "We're not doing *Blossom Time* or *The Student Prince*! We are doing a musical about 1959 for audiences of 1959. . . . It does not attack too many targets, it satirizes all of us, not just Fleet Street or the Church, but many other institutions. Slickey is a person striving for ideals in a commercial world. I am in it, you are in it." If some serious attempt had been made in the musical to render commercial values for what they are, all well and good, but, although Pelham says the opposite, far too many targets were attacked. A quick enumeration would include the nobility, the church, the press, the administration, success, sexual perverts, blood sports, corporal punishment, stately homes, women, anti-semites, anti-Negroes, pop-music, marriage, and M.P.s. With so many targets to aim at it is little wonder that there were no direct hits.

The plot was of the flimsiest nature, the background being the stately home of Lord and Lady Mancroft, the parents-in-law of Jack Oakham, alias Paul Slickey, who, unknown to them, is the infamous columnist of a scandal newspaper. Slickey is married to the Mancroft's daughter, Lesley, a successful business woman, but he sleeps with her sister Deirdre, whilst Deirdre's husband, Michael, a caricature of a prospective Conservative M.P., sleeps with Lesley. Most of this action takes place in the four-poster of the Marsden Room. The head of the family, Lord Mancroft, is ill, but should he last out a few more hours, then the family fortune will not fall into the hands of the State. Attended by his spiritual counsellor, Father Evilgreene, he looks like doing so, until a Mrs Giltedge-Whyte and her daughter Gillian arrive. Gillian is the result of a youthful affair between her mother and Lord Mancroft. In a final fling, Mancroft collapses whilst "performing" in another four-poster with Mrs Giltedge-Whyte! Whilst this has some humour, when one mixes in a love affair between Gillian and Terry Maroon, a pop idol and protégé of Lesley, and a mad brother George, the inventor of a sex change process, then the gâteau becomes just too sickly. The plot is more or less split into two, one half being about Mortlake Hall and the evasion of death duties, the other about the press and privacy, with Jack the only connexion between the two.

The songs are weak. With titles such as "The Income Tax Man", "The Mechanics of Success", or "Bring Back the Axe", no comment is needed to illuminate their content and most of them have very little to do with what is happening on the stage at that moment. If anything "saves" the show, it is the humour, but even this is very laboured when compared to that of the "public voice" Osborne. In this play the level is that of Slickey's comment about his wife:

SLICKEY. She's still mad about that story I wrote, about the Church Commissioners having invested money in her brassière company. . . . I simply suggested that the Church's one foundation might yet turn out to be an intimate under-garment in ear pink and mystery blue.[1]

Occasionally there is a flash of more intuitive humour:

DEIRDRE. Mummy's been so terribly brave.
JACK. Yes, she's always been a brave soul.
DEIRDRE. She has. I remember how she was when they gave away India. . . .[2]

[1] *W.P.S.*, p. 13.   [2] *Op. cit.*, p. 21.

Most of the political and social criticism is feeble and through-out the play the only passage which bears the true Osborne stamp, is that when Lesley describes her husband:

> LESLEY. All I know is that Jack has always suffered from excessive aspiration. There is a constant stain of endeavour underneath his emotional armpits. It throws off quite an unpleasant smell of sour ideals.[3]

The more obvious targets are not what they seem at first sight. Father Evilgreene, the piggish, corrupt "priest" is unfrocked when Mrs Giltedge-Whyte recognises him as an imposter. Thus what seemed a daring affront to the Church was nothing more than an indictment against clerical imposters. Paul Slickey who was supposed to be symbolic of the success-worship of our age is curiously soft-hearted and sympathetic, not happy with his job, and doubtful of the values of society; his only dishonest action in the play is to cheat during the "sex change". Slickey seems less controller than controlled. Our final impression of the gossip-monger of the gutter press, is that he is hard done by and forced into his position by the pressures of society.

Once again, the only characters who gain anything of our sympathy are the "remnants" of another age, the aristocrats themselves, Lord and Lady Mancroft. They provide the only human interest in the play, she forever arranging flowers, and he grasping his "last chance" with alacrity.

The script for *The World of Paul Slickey* is believed to date from pre- *Look Back in Anger* days, and one can fully understand why it had not been used earlier—the wonder being why 1959 was thought to be suitable for it! The show completely lacks that element of human warmth which unifies most of Osborne's work. Although it is about people, they lack vitality and compassion. In the familiar central role, Paul Slickey is never dominant enough or sufficiently human to capture our undivided attention. He is nothing, not good, not bad, neither a success nor a failure, he has little of importance to say and even less to do. With such a quantity of targets to attack

---

[3] *Op. cit.*, p. 50.

Osborne has little time or space to develop the case against Oakham, and he appears as some kind of idealistic hero. The whole affair was made even more unfortunate by the remarkable dedication Osborne gave the show:

> ... I dedicate this play to the liars and self-deceivers; ... this entertainment is dedicated to their boredom, their incomprehension, their distaste. It would be a sad error to raise a smile from them. A donkey with ears that could listen would no longer be a donkey; but that day may come when he is left behind because the other animals have learned to hear.[4]

At least one can say that "Slickey" did not commit the error of raising a smile, but we are left wondering who is the donkey?

II

If *The World of Paul Slickey* was noteworthy for its "dedication", John Osborne's television play, *A Subject of Scandal and Concern*, was no less remarkable for its "epilogue". This is a speech recited by the Narrator condemning the infamous "let us have an answer" brigade:

> This is a time when people demand from entertainment what they call a "solution". They expect to have their little solution rattling away down there in the centre of the play like a motto in a Christmas cracker. For those who seek information, it has been put before you. If it is meaning you are looking for, then you must start collecting for yourself. And what would you say is the moral then? If you are waiting for the commercial, it is probably this: you cannot live by bread alone. You must have jam—even if it is mixed with another man's blood. That's all. You may retire now. And if a mini-car is your particular mini-dream, then dream it. When your turn comes you will be called. Good night.[5]

Surely in this "epilogue" Osborne is underestimating the intelligence and the *feeling* of the "masses". Does he really believe that "they" or "we" are not capable of feeling or thinking? That mini-car may not seem very much, but given certain circumstances it can represent some significant achieve-

[4] *Op. cit.*, dedication.   [5] *S.S.C.*, pp. 76-7.

ment, or it can even be symbolic of a state of helplessness of which "we" are fully aware, and despise and loathe with as much feeling as Osborne, yet are powerless to change. It may well represent the realisation of our limitations—it does not necessarily imply our inability to see beyond the end of our noses. There is a pompousness about this epilogue which is alien to Osborne's self-appointed task to make us feel first and think later. We need facts and we need other people's views. We do not need to be told so emphatically what to do with them.

A Subject of Scandal and Concern is more documentary than play, with the numerous scenes, which are scarcely dramatic in themselves, linked together by a Narrator. The B.B.C. chose to use John Freeman, television's most famous "real life" narrator for this task, and did not give him a period setting costume. This technique served to heighten the alienation effect which the "injected" comment was likely to have in any case, and many viewers wrote in to complain that "it was hardly a play at all, but more like school". In fact the story is essentially straightforward, with ordinary dialogue and simple characterisation, and would have made perfectly good sense without the Narrator. It concerns the prosecution and trial of George Holyoake, the last man to be imprisoned in this country for the crime of blasphemy. Holyoake was a socialist lecturer, who, during question time at a meeting held in The Mechanics Hall, Cheltenham, was asked what he thought our duty to God to be. His answer constituted his blasphemy:

> HOLYOAKE.　Our national debt is a millstone around the poor man's neck, and our church and general religious institutions cost about twenty millions annually. Worship is expensive, and so I appeal to your heads and your pockets: are we not too poor to have God? If poor men cost the state as much, they would be put, like officers, on half pay. And while our present distress remains, it is wisest to do the same thing with Deity.[6]

When pushed further, he finally admitted to his questioner:

> I regard morality, but as for God, Mr Maitland, I cannot bring myself to believe in such a thing.

[6] *Op. cit.*, p. 16.

Holyoake had answered a religious question in a deliberately secular fashion, but the following day an article in the *Cheltenham Chronicle* deliberately misinterpreted this answer and demanded that the "socialist" be apprehended. Osborne comments on this through the Narrator:

> The methods of newspaper morality have changed very little.[7]

Despite a bad stutter and precious little knowledge of the law, George decides to defend himself when his trial begins. After a lame start he gets into his stride and does well, the weight of evidence is strongly in his favour and the Judge's summing up is tolerant. Yet when the jury return they announce a verdict of guilty and Holyoake is sentenced to six months' imprisonment. The trial scene certainly captures our attention, with George claiming freedom of conscience as a right of the individual within the rules of society.

In prison Holyoake is impassive to the news of the recantation of his friend Southwell, and refuses to react to the imploration of the Prison Chaplain. He seems content with his lot, and when his wife reproaches him about their under-nourished daughter's death and the bare funeral, he seems curiously unmoved:

> HOLYOAKE. I would rather regret my fortune—than—than be ashamed of my victory.[8]

This is the voice of the obsessed socialist, stubborn and unyielding. His cussedness has been gradually strengthened by the intolerance of others:

> PINCHING. Good-bye, Mr Holyoake. Unhappily the day has gone when we might send you *and* Mr Owen *and* Mr Southwell to the stake.[9]

Holyoake determines to stand against such people, he refuses the spiritual blackmail of the Chaplain, and obstinately demands a leather-bound Bible rather than accept the paperbacked prison issue. It is a demand indicative of his determination to preserve his individuality.

Osborne's Brechtian enthusiasm presumably encouraged

[7] *Op. cit.*, p. 18.   [8] *Op. cit.*, p. 44.   [9] *Op. cit.*, p. 22.

him to use the "narrator" method of exposition, which is a pity, for the effect was to distill interest. In its bare outline the story is dramatic, and one is left to wonder why Osborne did not adopt a more conventional dramatic form and write a larger and more intense play. Holyoake might have been another Luther, as it is, the script sacrifices the hero to the structure of the plot.

III

Plays for England was a double bill presented at the Royal Court in July, 1962. The first part, *The Blood of the Bambergs*, fared disastrously, but the second, *Under Plain Cover*, retrieved some of Osborne's reputation, and marked a departure for him into the fantasy world of Genet.

The Blood of the Bambergs, another satire, was based on the kind of farcical idea which needs a great deal of inventiveness to support it, a quality Osborne lacks. The plot deals with the substitution of an Australian press photographer for a Crown Prince who is killed in a car crash on the eve of his wedding. The photographer is the double of the deceased prince and is pressed into service by the Minister of Culture and his aides. Russell, the press man, accepts the situation, gratified by the thought of his newly found riches and the renowned sexual appetite of his royal bride-to-be. The hurried rehearsal of his part in the wedding is interrupted by the appearance of a "woman" who has hidden in the laundry chute, simply to get a glimpse of his "royal personage". Once again Osborne is disdainful of the masses, who are symbolically represented by the woman. She melodramatically exclaims:

> WOMAN. I worship you, I love you. You are my one and only God. Oh, Your Highness![10]

The exaggeration here, as elsewhere, is so heavy that the play loses any point it might have made. The woman eventually shoots herself, and a footman who has recognised Russell is shot. With these "obstacles" out of the way the

[10] *B.B.*, p. 60.

royal wedding proceeds in its full majesty. As one journalist comments:

> FIRST JOURNALIST. Happy is that land where the desire for symbols and display is expressed so harmlessly and yet so richly. Truly, an orb in the minster is worth a monster in orbit.[11]

The object of the satire was presumably royalty, but as in *The World of Paul Slickey*, the effect is weakened by a disclosure of identity—for where Father Evilgreene turned out *not* to be a priest, Russell it appears *is* of royal blood, being the outcome of a casual union many years earlier between his mother and the dead Prince's father! Thus the imposter is a "royal", and so perfectly presentable as Princess Melanie's husband. If the play's so-called attack hit anyone it was the television commentator Wimple who, it was pretty clear, was meant to be the late Richard Dimbleby. Wimple, in a long preamble to the "action", describes the scene in the cathedral on the eve of the wedding ceremony. Other "knuckle-close" references were made to certain public figures. Colonel Taft needed little "placing", and various Cabinet Ministers showed through the thinly veiled comments of Brown, Minister of Culture:

> BROWN. The only help we can look to is self-help. Now a lot of people think that by that we mean help yourself.[12]

The grapeshot was again too dispersed, aiming intermittently at the press, royalty, television, the church, the masses, politicians, and the trade unions. Most of the scorn is laid at the door of the press and television, for cheapening the image of royalty, a sentiment which seems in contradiction to Osborne's remarks about St Peter's and Buckingham Palace, made in his article for *Declaration*. Royalty in fact came out of the play quite well, with the sheer boredom of their life sympathetically rendered. Princess Melanie voiced these sentiments several times:

> MELANIE. My whole weary system is spinning around for ever like a royal satellite in a space of infinite and enduring boredom. Oh, my God, I am so bored![13]

---

[11] *Op. cit.*, p. 75.   [12] *Op. cit.*, p. 25.   [13] *Op. cit.*, p. 69.

I

Looked at as a whole, *the Blood of the Bambergs* is the feeblest play Osborne has allowed to reach the stage, resting as it does on a *pot-pourri* of hackneyed ideas about class, royalty, and religion. There is not enough humour to sustain the play throughout its two acts. The strong voice of a central character is entirely absent, and the play, by its failure to come alive, reminds us of the importance of Osborne's heroes, and of regarding him as a creator *par excellence* of dramatic lead parts.

IV

The second half of *Plays for England* was *Under Plain Cover*, a short play examining the adjustments made by a young married couple who act a series of sado-masochistic fantasies. Ostensibly the play is an attack upon the intrusion of the Press into the sphere of private relationships. Tim and Jenny are, to the outside world, a perfectly normal, happily married couple, and only the postman who is forever delivering parcels to their house, "under plain cover", could doubt the normality of their life. The play opens with a series of set-pieces in which the couple indulge their love of dressing up, by playing parts in fantasy situations they create themselves—a doctor and his maid, a boxer and a girl guide, a ton-up boy and a pregnant bride. First one partner dominates, then the other. The 1930s scene is particularly well presented, Tim aristocratically domineering, Jenny subservient and whimpering:

> JENNY. My dad'll understand—especially when I tell him the kind of man you are. I'll get another job.
> TIM. It's the nineteen thirties.[14]

The couple have a tremendous enthusiasm for their parts, and these scenes have an unforced naturalness about them which is quite enthralling. The farcical inventiveness so sadly lacking in the playwright's attempted satires is presented here, especially in a long episode where Tim and Jenny rhapsodise about knickers. Every conceivable description is applied to the subject, notably several reviews of Osborne's earlier plays:

> TIM. As for the garment itself. Well, construction is weak of course . . . the final gesture is totally inadequate . . . not

[14] *U.P.C.*, p. 95.

without quality . . . the reason for the elastic is never clearly
or adequately explained.[15]

This suburban version of Genet is disturbed by the appearance
of Stanley, a reporter, whose editor has discovered that the
couple are, in fact, brother and sister.

The second half of the play tails off badly, for Osborne's
incessant desire to attack the press has intruded and destroyed
the innocence of the opening scenes. Both style and subject
change completely. Stanley breaks the news to the couple,
separates them, and marries Jenny off within a fortnight to
another young man, he even manages to get Tim invited to the
wedding! Jenny's second marriage fails and the play ends with
Tim and Jenny reconciled, living secretly together, and a broken
Stanley trying unsuccessfully to talk to them and so screw out
another sensational story.

What does Osborne mean by all this? Is he claiming that
the ordinary journalist is unable to appreciate human com-
plexity? Does he intend there to be a contrast between the
halves of the plays? Or is he simply trying to show that the truth
is deliberately distorted by the press for their own ends? The
morality of the *Cheltenham Chronicle*, is on par with that of
Stanley, who even cheats his colleagues by pretending not to
bid for the postman's "exclusive" story, telling the others that
he does not believe "in all this trading in human beings".

Our final impression of the play is that what was once a
private "working" relationship between two lovers is broken
by the squalid intrusion of the gutter press—emotional
expression is once more restricted. The fantasy sequences offer
a glimpse into a part of life which is only occasionally studied,
and even more rarely discussed. John Taylor interpreted the
play as:

> a sort of fourth act to *Look Back in Anger*, in which Jimmy and
> Alison have tired of Bears and Squirrels and gone on to a few
> more sophisticated party games. . . . And as a result of their
> fantasies and fetishes they are happy, well-adjusted, efficient
> parents and, as far as the outside world is concerned, just what
> the postman calls them, a nice ordinary couple. Indeed,

[15] *Op. cit.*, p. 117.

absolutely they are just that: they have a marriage which works: they merely externalize changes in the emotional balance of a power and make positive use of them where others experience them only as a bug-bear and a puzzlement.[16]

Under Plain Cover would have been best left as a brief excursion into the fantasy world of Tim and Jenny, rather than padded out into an unsatisfactory play. It is interesting to contrast the scenes of their life together at the beginning of the play, with the way in which the journalist's narrative rushes us through nine years, in which the couple become little more than puppets. It is, of course, quite possible, and not at all abstruse, to think of the play as an attempt to show the necessity for diversion owing to the boredom of modern suburban marriage. With this interpretation the play becomes closer to drama than to psychiatric therapy.

V

A Bond Honoured was suggested to Osborne by Kenneth Tynan, Literary Manager of the National Theatre. It is based on Lope de Vega's *La Fianza Satisfecha*. The adaptation retains the sense of cruelty of the original, exposing the innermost feelings of Leonido, a man of exceptional violence and sadism. We see this in his relationship with his sister, Marcela, with whom in Osborne's play he commits incest, and with his father, Gerardo, whom he despises. Even his sleepy servant, Tizon, is brutally maltreated in a long opening scene, where Osborne begins his exposition of Leonido's character.

The play takes on the appearance of a ritual. The players are grouped in a circle, and as they become concerned in the action they emerge from the shadows to take their place alongside Leonido, and having done so, fade back into the ring. There is a pent-up imprisoned animality about the proceedings, as the depths of individual will and obsession are plumbed. We ask ourselves how satanic can Leonido become without needing to meet his conscience. His aim is to locate the boundaries of human possibility.

One difficulty in comprehending *A Bond Honoured* is that of

[16] J. R. Taylor, *Anger and After*. London, 1963, p. 56.

casting oneself back to a period when the idea of Christ and his teachings were necessarily accepted by society, and where it was almost impossible to exist, as Leonido did, wearing Moorish clothes, pillaging his father's heart, and defiling his sister. The meaning of the Lope de Vega play rests on the question of when, and how, God would redress the balance against Leonido.

As far as the plot of Osborne's play is concerned, Leonido rapes his sister on the eve of her marriage to Dionisio, though the word "rape" is rather too strong, for their sexual attraction is mutual. Marcela is not perturbed by her brother's remarks about her future husband and she tells her brother, in half-amusement, that Dionisio:

> MARCELA. ... complains you have lied all over Sicily that he's a bastard. That his mother was a whore and a crone and the only woman who has died in childbed of old age.[17]

When Leonido's father reproaches him for "treading upon his sister's bridal gown", the son is rude and contemptuous:

> LEONIDO. I say that clapper tongue of yours has deafened you inside that hollow bell.[18]

Likewise he has no respect for, or fear of, Dionisio, his future brother-in-law, whom he despises as being, "as lawful as an endless sermon". In a pique of sadistic spite and jealousy he visits Marcela on her actual wedding night, "to spoil the bride's sleep". As they talk Marcela hears her husband coming. He enters as Leonido tries to strip off his sister's nightgown; the men duel, Dionisio falls to the ground, and as Leonido leaves, he strikes Marcela with his sword. Outside in the garden Leonido meets his servant Tizon, who asks:

> TIZON. Have you no feeling? Even for the reckoning?
> LEONIDO. I have God's credit for the moment. Let him settle up for me, and send in his account when he wants to.[19]

This is the "bond" to be honoured.

Leonido is found asleep on the beach by some raiding Moors, but defeats them in a short battle. The Moor King, Berlebeyo, explains that he was seeking to capture a Christian hostage to

[17] *B.H.*, p. 24.   [18] *Op. cit.*, p. 26.   [19] *Op. cit.*, p. 33.

give to the woman he loves but cannot please. This bizarre situation appeals to Leonido, and he accepts the offer to go with the Moors to Tunis. He puts on Moorish robes instructing Tizon to go to his father, Gerardo, and tell him:

> LEONIDO. I renounce his blood. Also his God, his law, the baptism and the sacrament, oh yes, and the Passion of Death. I think I shall follow Mahomet.[20]

Lidora, the woman the Moor King loves, ironically falls in love with Leonido, but her feelings are not returned, for the "hero" tells her she is "no more beautiful than some overheated whelp trailing strangers in the bazaar". Later when other Christians are captured they turn out to be Gerardo, Marcela, and Tizon, who are welcomed by Lidora; Leonido resents their intrusion, scornful of their servility to the Moors and sinking even deeper into his own viciousness, he stabs out his father's eyes; and, when frustrated from killing Gerardo, he rushes out threatening to burn Tunis.

The bond tightens and Leonido begins to realise his isolation and admits to a mysterious voice which beckons him:

> LEONIDO. My imprint will have died out of all hearts inside a month. Discard. A discard.[21]

The voice is replaced by the symbolic Shepherd (in the original play Christ) telling Leonido of the debt he owes. The account is about to be settled. Leonido, weary and resigned, acknowledges that he is overspent, and tells the Shepherd that he shall have his life to settle the debt. In Osborne's play Leonido is not overawed by Christ, as he was in Lope de Vega's.

The others find him, he fights but soon throws down his sword, and begs forgiveness of his father and sister. The plot thickens melodramatically when he reveals that he once raped his own mother, that the child was carried off by a bear, and that when he returned from chasing the animal he found a baby, Marcela. Leonido absent-mindedly recalls that he stabbed his mother—at this he is dragged out and hanged. King Berbeleyo then reads a letter written by his deceased father

[20] *Op. cit.*, p. 39.   [21] *Op. cit.*, p. 57.

which explains how the old King, whilst hunting in Sicily some years before, had rescued a Christian baby girl, Lidora, from a bear and brought her home. Thus Lidora is Marcela's long lost sister. The King decides to set them all free, and they take Leonido's body to Sicily, but not until Tizon the servant has stabbed it. The play seems so false towards the end that the "pantomime" ending is almost appropriate, indeed a tune to end with:

> Tizon. Well, King, he played a good tune on vituperation. It may not be a bond honoured, but it's a tune of sorts to end with.[22]

Once more we find ourselves asking what did Osborne mean by this play? Can it be regarded as anything more than an experience. Could the Lope de Vega play have any meaning for a contemporary audience? Osborne states that he was fascinated by the dialectic with the principal character of the Lope de Vega original, and by the Christian frame-work of the play. One of the most memorable passages of the Osborne reconstruction is that in which Tizon tries to explain the essence of Christianity to Lidora. She is surprised at the fact that a Christian's salvation depends upon only Ten Commandments, and that man can be mortal and immortal at the same time. Reminiscent of Luther, this is the more familiar Osborne speaking. The concentration upon the single solitary character is another trademark, as is the weakness of the minor characterisation. The vehemence of the life portrayed might conceivably have made *A Bond Honoured* a "public voice" play: but the second half of the play is too elaborately devised and the story becomes unfeasible, diluting the exploration of violence which preceded it. Two phrases in the Osborne play suggest that some contemporary relevance might have been intended; one is "our shrinking possibilities", the other, "our overprotected island". These should not be mistaken as pertinent to Great Britain, for the phrases have a wider significance. In the play they referred to the restrictive adherence to the Catholic rule of life. What Leonido has done is to break free from all restriction. He has but one

[22] *Op. cit.*, p. 62.

bond—to God.   He owes no allegiance to any man or anything on earth.   He renounces his father, his blood, his church.
His inordinate violence represents the extremes to which we
might go, were we free of the conventions of our time.   Once
again we see the rejection of society's code of behaviour and
belief, and a solitary individual seeking an answer for himself.
Yet because of its obsessional violence, its lack of widespread
general social criticism, and the absence of the "soliloquy",
we may justifiably classify the play as a "private voice" work.
In reality it is an outsider—a projection of Osborne's theme into
the world of "super-expressionism".

VII

Themes

THAT Osborne chooses to express his opinions through the situation and words of a finely drawn central character is more a matter of technique than any outsize transference of personal self to that character. There is by the very nature of life a close connexion between an artist and his work; it would be a strange writer indeed whose literary characters do not express, in some form or another, what he himself believes. Moreover, at an Osborne play, the involvement of the audience is usually so intense that we could legitimately claim an "autobiographical transference" on the part of most people present.

His characters undergo, before our eyes, a process of self-acceptance which is at the same time a plea for individual responsibility and freedom. The heroes, aware of their plight, despair, and eventually attain full self-expression. They are people of sensitivity, their goodwill blunted by exposure to society, unable to do more than protest ineffectually at what is happening to them. Lacking the power to alter the scheme of things or even their own small part in that scheme, they establish some kind of repetitive pattern in their lives, which in turn drives others away. Thus, left on the sidelines, they warn others by means of vibrant monologues to beware of a similar fate. In their speeches we hear Osborne's "public" voice, with all its obsessions and quirks, its beliefs and disappointments, its encouragement and its warning. Whatever the play, the voice is the same:

> . . . whether the scene is a provincial attic or a stately home, whether the mask is that of an ageing music-hall comic, or a German monk, the voice is the voice of the dramatist. The text is both the imprint of Mr Osborne's own obsessions and angers, his personal fantasies and his public commitments. His men are all maimed in some way—beat up veterans of the

sex war or the class war—and the best they hope for is to escape the final horror of emasculation. It is this identification with the self-punishing martyr which makes John Osborne's work unique in the modern theatre, at once embarrassing and exhilarating, simultaneously, a belch of defiance and a cry for help.[1]

Osborne's heroes are alone, and worse, they know it:

> JIMMY. The heaviest, strongest creatures in the world seem to be the loneliest.[2]

So aware are they of their *difference* that they repeatedly see their own lives and problems in those of others. Bill Maitland mirrors his own feelings when he says to his client Marples:

> BILL. ... Let's be quite honest about it, and you feel you are gradually being deserted and isolated.[3]

The final fear of Osborne must be that no one will listen—he does care and any number of Archie's songs will not hide the fact, nor will Frank's protests that "we've only got ourselves and must think of number one". Repeatedly the heroes plead not to be left alone. George Dillon is prepared to sacrifice himself to prevent this happening, and prefers the "warmth" of the Elliot family to creative isolation. Laurie we know, will need Annie's love and respect. Even Luther cannot go it alone forever, and seeks affection in the arms of his nun.

Much of the heroes' "difference" is deliberately caused, for they seek to satisfy their individual conscience before that of society. Whilst Luther cries "I am alone, I am alone, and against myself" his choice is deliberate, so is that of George Holyoake, whose words emphasise his awareness of his "difference":

> HOLYOAKE. If you think it right to differ from the times and to make a stand for any valuable points of morals, do it, however rustic, however antiquated it may appear. Do it, not for insolence, but seriously. As a man who wore the soul of his own in his bosom—and did not wait till it was breathed into him by the breath of fashion.[4]

---

[1] *Sunday Telegraph*, 13 Sep. 1964.   [2] *L.B.A.*, p. 94.
[3] *I.E.*, p. 92.   [4] *S.S.C.*, p. 18.

It is this "soul of their own" which has caused trouble to the heroes, they are not prepared to accept second best, or other people's values, and search for their own levels of satisfaction, in doing so they become "different", apart from the herd. It is an incredible reflexion about life that these sentiments, which can only be regarded as admirable, should lead to such despair and to such isolation. Is Osborne like Luther: "the only one to see all this and suffer"?

The two least likeable characters, Redl and Leonido, are the heroes who seem to satisfy their needs most adequately, yet both die. Redl seeks to cure his personal loneliness by becoming a practising homosexual. Advocate Kunz describes their mutual plight when he talks of the drag-ball as:

> BARON. . . . a place for people to come together. People who are often in their everyday lives, rather lonely and even miserable and feel hunted. . . .[5]

Redl refuses to be hunted, and in admitting his "queerness", and by enjoying his real self, condemns himself in the eyes of society—yet is now free to enjoy the full expression of his true nature. He is able to live a complete life, as *he* wants and not as others want him to.

Leonido, in his turn, renounces his bond to all that which normally governs life: family, church, society. He admits to one debt and one debt only. Revelling in his ability to inflict pain, he reaches to the depths of depravity, triumphantly claiming:

> LEONIDO. A bastard's common too, but a bastard you see's separate, a weed, often strong, quite powerful.[6]

His isolation is intentional. Having completely freed himself from the conventional life, he can explore the furthermost limits of humanity—he might equally have been an incredibly good man.

Thus both Redl and Leonido, by their complete rejection of the usual "conditions of life" escape the pain and loneliness

[5] *P.M.*, p. 85.   [6] *B.H.*, p. 24-5.

of the "normal" heroes. For whilst both are "separate" their deliberate decision has enabled them to control the situation, unlike the others, who permit the situation to control them.

The theme of isolation is, I think, the least obsessive and yet the most important of Osborne's themes. It is not by the quotation of all those phrases, "I want to be left alone", that we can show its significance, though this does witness its frequent occurrence; rather we can prove it by asking ourselves, what is Osborne's intention? He is trying to make us think about the nature of our existence. Osborne's plays are experiences, not lessons with questions and answers, though we should not deny that they provoke questions and hence answers, nor that he has made it obvious what the answer should be.

What then do the plays suggest? They suggest that there is something wrong with a society which "isolates" human beings who simply want to be *themselves*, to complete their own development, and not necessarily accept that which society forces upon them. If we have the courage to realise ourselves, then we shall also probably become isolated. For those with the half-courage of Jimmy, George, Bill, and Laurie the pain of needing to opt in and out of society will be desperate. Aware of their difference, angry at the injustice they see around them, but helpless to change it and desperate for recognition and love, they despair, to end alone and defeated. Osborne's purpose is to imply the need for change, any change, so that this vicious circle might not complete itself. The anger which was so apparent in the plays is an expression of the heroes' aversion to a life without worthwhile belief or hope. "To be angry is to care", and Osborne's anger is certainly one that stems from love. His anger is rarely concentrated in one direction for any length of time. Most of the plays are in the aggressively first person, and the attacks are uncontrolled and often irrational. Jimmy Porter earned the title "angry young man" for Osborne, and he certainly was opposed to many aspects of modern life, striking out, in turn, at the church, the press, the bomb, the older generation, women, marriage, sex, and the "Establishment". Yet one should remember that Jimmy's anger is not simply revenge for the injustices he has suffered. He is capable of vicarious suffering, and much of his anger does indeed come from his love of others and his helplessness to change things:

> JIMMY. You see, I learnt at an early age what it is to be angry—angry and helpless. And I can never forget it.[7]

Look Back in Anger is not a play about anger, it is about feelings, about despair, and Jimmy Porter has a compassion which many have denied him in their haste to decry his "irresponsible" spite and loathing. Much of his anger is tempered by a plea for "justice". It is not malicious, but concentrates on demonstrating the injustice of the world. The direct objects of his attack are not the focus of any subjective personal hate on Jimmy's behalf.

Not all of Osborne's characters possess this type of anger. Bill Maitland is making a last stand against society, against insensitivity. He deplores the materialistic ends of most of his fellows, and their acceptance of the trivial. Sarcastically he tries to ridicule them: "Jones entering the Promised Land in his mini". But Bill is apathetic, almost beyond anger, for he is out of touch with those around him; his empathy gone, he is reduced to petty personal gibes, like describing his mistress' father as a "little intellectual monkey" chattering away about Copernicus on the telly. His feelings have retracted, only occasionally does Maitland lash out in real anger, and then only when his own position is menaced:

> BILL. .... Look at this dozy bastard: Britain's position in the world. Screw that. What about my position?[8]

Bill's anger is one that causes little offence, he is simply trying to find a way round the banality of it all. His anger, what there is of it, is justified by the tepid response of those around him.

Archie Rice is likewise beyond anger in the aggressive "Porter" sense. He leaves that kind of feeling to the young, to his children. Jean is the mouthpiece Osborne uses in *The Entertainer* to express his disgust with our self-complacency:

> JEAN. Everbody's tired, everybody's standing about loitering without any intent whatsoever, waiting to be picked up by whatever they may allow to happen to us next.[9]

---

[7] *L.B.A.*, p. 58.   [8] *I.E.*, p. 29.   [9] *E.*, p. 75.

Archie, by way of contrast, is angry because of his supposed burden. The British theatre is epitomised in his person, he is a symbol of its state of decay, and of our decay. When he protests, it is a sarcastic note in the margin, that is all, for he knows his effort is useless. As he cynically tells his wife:

> ARCHIE. This is a Welfare State, my darling heart. Nobody wants, and nobody goes without, all are provided for. . . .[10]

If Archie is beyond anger and comment, George Dillon isn't, yet the anger is again one of care, care for himself and his fellow beings. George protests at what fate has in store for him when he asks Ruth:

> GEORGE. Have you looked at them? Have you listened to them? They don't merely act and talk like caricatures, they are caricatures! That's what's so terrifying. . . . They think in clichés, they talk in them, they even feel in them. . . .[11]

This description of the Elliot family is George's way of warning himself not to accept their standards. It is also a warning to us. This is not petulant anger, it is a terrifying awareness of what life could become, and an impotent protest against it, a cry for help as he is sucked under.

Anger can be expressed in many ways: in the shouts of the Elliot household, "Slut! Slut! Slut!"; in the rantings of Jimmy Porter, "That's my wife. That's her isn't it?", or in the theological disgust of Luther at the sale of indulgences. The method of expression may be the repetitive curse, the single cutting remarks, or the rambling monologue. Osborne explores many methods, but underlying the theme of anger, as expressed in his plays, is his unending concern to suggest the idea of something better, a dream of a more perfect existence.

Even in his low-keyed *For the Meantime* plays Osborne's anger is still evident, but his pet hates are now only mildly castigated. His characters are more disillusioned than defeated, indeed they have achieved some measure of worldy success but only by the sacrifice of their integrity. There is a stronger air of nihilism and only occasionally does the more bracing Osborne

[10] *Op. cit.*, p. 53.   [11] *E.G.D.*, p. 58.

invective burst through, as it does when Laurie bitterly condemns K.L.:

> LAURIE. Where does he get the damned energy and duplicity? Where? He's tried to split us up but here we are in Amsterdam. He has made himself the endless object of speculation. Useful to him but humiliating for us. Well, no more, my friend. We will no longer be useful to you and be put up and be put down. We deserve a little better, not much but better. We have been your friends. Your stock in trade is marked down *and* your blackmailing sneering, your callousness, your malingery, your emotional gunslinging, your shooting in the dark places of affection. You trade on the forbearance, kindliness and talent of your friends. Go on, go on playing the big market of all those meretricious ambition hankers, plodding hirelings, grafters and intriguers. I simply hope tonight that you are alone—I know you won't be. But I hope, at least, you will feel alone, alone as I feel it, as we all in our time feel it, without burdening our friends. I hope the G.P.O. telephone system is collapsed, that your chauffeur is dead, and the housekeeper drunk and that there isn't one con-man, camp follower, eunuch, pimp, mercenary, or procurer of all things possible or one globe trotting bum boy at your side to pour you a drink on this dark January evening. . . .[12]

Laurie quivers with anger as he damns his boss, and in this Porteresque monologue Osborne's desire for something better for us all is clearly evident, as is his ultimate fear, loneliness—for his greatest curse is to thrust the threat of isolation in K.L.'s face.

A target which Osborne repeatedly attacks and without qualification is the Press. The dedication to *The World of Paul Slickey* is quite extraordinary:

> No one has ever dedicated a string quartet to a donkey although books have been dedicated to critics. I dedicate this play to the liars and self-deceivers; to those who daily deal out treachery; to those who handle their professions as instruments of debasement; to those who, for a salary cheque and less, successfully betray my country, and those who will do it for no inducement at all.[13]

[12] *H.A.*, p. 117.   [13] *W.P.S.*, dedication.

Apart from the fact that this sounds more like a "chauvinistic press editorial" than part of a play, it is a violent comment about press morality. Osborne's theme of Press intrusion is his silliest and most obsessive. The "newspaper scenes" of *The World of Paul Slickey* are intended to echo the sentiment of this "dedication", and to illustrate the passionate bankruptcy of the Press in their drive for organised triviality. This is obvious Osborne anger, but seems much less worthy, being simple revenge, tit-for-tat. That the critics use the same methods we need not deny, and that they should be criticised is both legitimate and necessary: but a more rational approach would surely illustrate their frailty more emphatically. Osborne's hobby-horse has rather run away with him here, and if he is to succeed in arousing society and to get it thinking idealistically, then he must take firmer grip of the reins. As Coleridge said, "Freedom is a very fine horse to ride, but to ride somewhere".

Under Plain Cover affords further evidence of this obsession of Osborne's for slamming the gutter press, and he spends unconstructive time describing the squalid bidding by the "journalists" for the postman's "exclusive" story about Tim and Jenny. The ending, where the couple are happily reunited, whilst the miserably drunk and defeated Stanley begs to talk to them, seems to afford Osborne curious pleasure. In his later plays he appears to have shifted his position slightly. Easing up, as it were, on the lower realms of writing he addresses himself to the "phoney" artist. Pamela in *Time Present* emphasises the banality of many playwrights:

> PAMELA. People sit around and make up Freudian epigrams about one another. It's written by someone thinking about writing it instead of thinking about whatever it's about.[14]

If the press is one target for Osborne's anger, class and the Establishment are others. In fact, we could validly state that isolation and anger are the major themes of his plays, whilst the causes of much of that anger are secondary themes: class, religion, the Establishment, boredom, and what might be called the "mini-mind". Another important theme is that of the ambivalent nostalgia which is present in most of Osborne's

[14] *T.P.*, p. 73.

work. Some minor themes occur such as the sense of culpability and the fear of death, but they are closer to, and can be grouped within the general conception of isolation.

Class awareness is certainly a common feature of Osborne's contemporary plays. *Look Back in Anger* was very much concerned with the class struggle, and Jimmy Porter seemed to revel in that battle, "a young man without money, background or even looks, who was not going to be intimidated because of that". He has the nerve to be outspoken on all subjects, even those normally the preserve of the upper classes. He is even articulate about class, describing Helena as one of Alison's "posh girl friends with lots of money and no brains". Yet he is unsatisfied with his own class background and is the first to admit this, calling his university white tile rather than red brick! Thus his attitude is to be one of anger against those who have been dealt the aces of the class hand, the Nigels and the Bishops of Bromley, all those in fact who make the mistake of thinking:

> JIMMY. . . . that because Hugh's mother was a deprived ignorant old woman, who said all the wrong things in all the wrong places, she couldn't be taken seriously.[15]

Jimmy has no patience with these people, to him they inhabit "enemy territory" and he has no public school scruples in dealing with them. He would, we feel sure, refuse to join a class capable of a dismissal so dispassionate as that afforded to Hugh's mother.

Like Jimmy Porter, Archie Rice is not capable of a change in allegiance and refuses to accept his brother's offer of a new life in Canada, he does not wish to join the middle classes. Archie enjoys poking fun at the well-to-do, yet like Jimmy Porter, he is also willing to ridicule his own kind when they "ape" the manners of others. Of his wife's liking for gin and Dubonnet, he remarks how "U" she thinks she is when she drinks it. The songs of *The Entertainer* pursue their own class war, especially Frank's refrain:

> . . . . Those playing fields of Eton
> Have really got us beaten. . . . .[16]

[15] *L.B.A.*, p. 73.   [16] *E.*, p. 74.

Eton features in *The World of Paul Slickey*, where numerous sallies are made at the class barrier. Michael, Slickey's brother-in-law, is the very epitome of what Osborne conceives as the upper class moron. Michael, a prospective Conservative M.P., bases his election campaign on the idea of giving "the bomb" to the Germans. He believes his constituency, because it was erased by bombing in the last war, must be interested in foreign affairs! Michael is so "wet" that even Lady Mancroft makes excuses for him:

> LADY MANCROFT. I do think you ought to remember Michael has been denied many of the advantages that fall to more fortunate men.
>
> DEIRDRE. I wouldn't call Eton, Oxford and the Guards exactly liabilities.
>
> LADY MANCROFT. Those things are hardly advantages any more than arms and legs are. . . .[17]

We are reminded here of the futility of even trying to change the order of things. Lady Mancroft knows the prerogative of her kind. Michael is depicted with some humour by Osborne and this tends to take the sting out of his more banal remarks:

> MICHAEL. I am prepared to go to the House of Lords. Thank goodness there are some representatives of the people left who have their genuine interest at heart![18]

Osborne can be equally cruel to the working classes and his sets for the play *Epitaph for George Dillon* were particularly damning, complete with flying plaster ducks, cocktail cabinet, and the ever present pastel-tinted wedding photograph. This is as obvious a caricature as that of Colonel Taft in *The Blood of the Bambergs*. These caricatures are too pointed to be taken seriously and suggest that Osborne is not worried with the injustice of class as such, but is more concerned with the class structure as an obstacle to that personal realisation he thinks our true aim. Thus he seizes every opportunity to ridicule "class" and the social status "ladder". Consequently we get the exaggerated master and maid sequence in *Under Plain Cover*, in which the upper class gentleman adopts an attitude of "I said you wait,

---

[17] *W.P.S*, p. 32. [18] *Op. cit.*, p. 27.

you horrible little skivvy", whilst the servant sniffs and mumbles in supposed lower class fashion.

Whilst class is an obvious theme in the contemporary plays we should not presume that it is absent from the "historical" plays. In *Luther*, Martin's father makes several significant remarks about class, and the Knight criticises the cut-rate nobility and rich layabouts who squeezed every penny out of the peasants. He asks Martin whether all men are redeemed by Christ's blood or just the Princes! Not only did sixteenth-century Germany have its class divisions, but nineteenth-century Austria too, for in *A Patriot for Me* the army is depicted as a place of privilege, full of short cuts for those who apparently don't deserve it.

Curiously Osborne seems to have accepted the existence of those barriers, for in the hapless plight of most of his heroes he might well be saying, "there is the class wall, struggle as you might, you won't scale it, so why not accept it?" This is especially true of his latest plays *Time Present* and *The Hotel in Amsterdam*. One "hero", Pamela, claims in fact to be a high Tory, and the class element is almost totally absent in these works.

It is also important for us to remember the climate of the period when the "class warfare" plays were written, for today, the sets especially, with their ironing boards and plaster ducks, seem very dated; and we can see in *Time Present* and *The Hotel in Amsterdam* a definite adjustment in Osborne's position. He now seems resigned to a "personal escape" answer to the class problem.

That Osborne is concerned with religion is apparent and obvious from the fact that two of his plays *Luther* and *A Subject of Scandal and Concern* examine the question of religious conscience and the nature of belief. In Osborne's other plays religion is integral to the Establishment theme rather than tackled as a subject in itself. *The Entertainer* provides the most telling expression of Osborne's attitude to this subject and stresses the irrelevance of dogma in today's environment. Jean rebuffs her fiancé's claims for a good life, by asking him:

> JEAN. Have you ever got on a railway train here, got on a train from Birmingham to West Hartlepool? Or gone from

Manchester to Warrington or Widnes. And you get out, you go down the street, and on one side maybe is a chemical works, and on the other side is the railway goods yard. Some kids are playing in the street, and you walk up to some woman standing on her doorstep. It isn't a doorstep really because you can walk straight from the street into her front room. What can you say to her? What real piece of information, what message can you give to her? Do you say Madam, d'you know that Jesus died on the Cross for you?[19]

This is a damning criticism of our social system and of the Church. What attempt, it asks, has the Church made to answer the problems of today, or even to "belong" to this world? The same point is flippantly made in *The World of Paul Slickey*, when Deirdre tells her mother that whilst she has to pay tax at 19/6 in the pound, she finds the idea of a Divine Providence rather laughable. For Osborne religious bodies are shirking the issue; they do not face the moral questions of today, but are content to rest quietly in the past. He is not questioning the need for faith, but rather suggesting that we have been let down by the "instruments" of that faith. Lady Mancroft's answer to Deirdre is very much to the point:

DEIRDRE. It seems to me that Daddy had a genius for finding reasons for not doing things.
LADY MANCROFT. Of course dear, that is the very basis of all religions.[20]

Osborne attacks the choir but not the hymn, his concern is with the basis of belief rather than the "essential beauty of the ceremonial". It is a plea for more religion, not less. A protest at the ornamentation so hilariously sent up in *Inadmissible Evidence*, where Bill Maitland imagines his own cremation:

BILL. . . . all that G-plan light oak and electrical department brass fittings and spanking new magenta hassocks. And the pink curate sending you off at thirty bob a head as I go rattling on little rails behind him and disappear like a truck on the ghost train at Dreamland, in the Amusement Park, behind the black curtains, and all that noise.[21]

Evelyn Waugh had no surer touch than this.

[19] *E.*, p. 84-5.   [20] *W.P.S.*, p. 73.   [21] *I.E.*, p. 85.

Osborne ridicules royalty more cruelly than he does religion, for he suggests that religion has some value but that a monarchic system in a socialist country is, at best, a strange paradox. Osborne attaches no blame to the "royal personages" themselves, sympathising with what he calls " royal satellite in a space of infinite and enduring boredom". His satire is directed against those who support such nonsense, against the glibness of the smooth television commentator in *The Blood of the Bambergs*: "... we shall be privileged to watch the most solemn occasion in our national life—a royal wedding". This is the pathetic idolatry which Osborne wishes to expose, and he does so in his usual fashion, bright splashy waves of words focusing our attention on the triviality of it all. Now and then a more serious note creeps into the general tone, when he asks, via Jean in *The Entertainer*, "is it really just for the sake of a gloved hand waving at you from a golden coach?'. His private views are clear enough, for he spoke on the subject in *Declaration*:

> I have called Royalty religion the "national swill" because it is poisonous, what an old vegetarian I used to know would call "foodless food", or, as Orwell might have put it, the leader writers and the bribed gossip mongers have only to rattle their sticks in the royalty bucket for most of their readers to put their heads down in this trough of Queen worship, their tails turned against the world. It doesn't seem as funny anymore![22]

This is an attack on us. Osborne asks "What kind of symbols do we live by? Are they truthful and worthwhile?"

The Government is subject to the same examination, and once again we are ridiculed for being fobbed-off with Ministerial statements like "the man in the street. I know him, he knows me", or "... our race is not yet run and it is not yet lost". In the play, *The Blood of the Bambergs*, Osborne overstates his point about triviality by equating the cost of a year's royal occasions to the lost opportunity for the Government to build 27 secondary modern schools and 1,200,000 houses! This anti-Government theme is common to all his contemporary plays; from Jimmy Porter's "platitudes from out of space" to Bill Maitland's— "Naylor Report, failure report..." and Pamela's "striding into

[22] John Osborne, "They Call it Cricket". *Declaration*, ed. T. Masschler, p. 68

the seventies. I haven't got used to hobbling about in the sixties yet''.

What Osborne feels up against are the obstacles society has erected to prevent the truth becoming clear. He is protesting at the irrelevances with which we obscure our personal expression. Hence his repetitive outcries against the aristocracy, royalty, the church, the press, and politicians, against anything in fact, which obstructs the fullest expression of life. This concept is given bitter expression in *The World of Paul Slickey*:

> And you will say to the ultimate journalist, as he leans unsteadily against the bar of deceit, as he asks the questions that prevent real questions being asked. . . .[23]

One could imagine what Osborne would ask! Whatever it would be, almost certainly it would contain a request to the journalists to throw away their banner headlines: "I MARRIED MY BROTHER"; to accept the passing of the Empire; to acknowledge our hypocrisy; to forget the petty trivialities with which we seem content to concern ourselves; and to ask, to ask repeatedly, the real questions. Laurie's damning of his grasping relatives is equally to the point and more than appropriate:

> LAURIE. They're not quite funny, Annie. They're greedy, calculating, stupid and totally without questions.[24]

This is a plea for responsibility and for honesty, an encouragement to apply ourselves to seek values worthy of imaginative human beings. Without this honesty we can only be preoccupied with material gain, and a morbid longing for a past era when values were, if not any better, at least not questioned.

This longing for the past is the central contradiction in Osborne's work. In his acceptance of a past which often had poorer standards than those of a present which he *does not* accept. He has pity for Alison's father, yet the Colonel represents a much more entrenched class position than that which Jimmy Porter opposes in *Look Back in Anger*. The nostalgia is usually represented by one of the "older generation"

---

[23] *W.P.S.*, p. 28.   [24] *A.A.*, p 127.

or else it takes the form of a longing by the hero for the stability of a forgotten order. Alison's father, the Colonel, and Archie's father, Billy, immediately spring to mind as does Pamela's father, Orme. The Colonel paraphrases this sentimentality when he reminisces:

> COLONEL. ... That was my world and I loved it, all of it. ....
> When I think of it now it seems like a dream. If only it
> could have gone on forever. ....[25]

Osborne is most sympathetic in his treatment of the "remnants"; his stage instructions for the portrayal of Billy Rice are themselves an exercise in nostalgia; "When he (Billy) speaks it is with a dignified Edwardian diction. ... Indeed it is not an accent of class but of period. One does not hear it often now". The playwright even grants these characters words, which whilst true to character, are directly opposed to his own sentiments. Billy Rice is constantly critical of the present day, and at one point reminds the younger generation that in his day, "one Britisher could always take on half a dozen of that kind", something which can hardly be Osborne's own belief. Gideon Orme's theatre has long since died but throughout *Time Present* his presence is with us through his daughter Pamela, who has derived from him a strict code of behaviour and self-sufficiency.

Throughout Osborne's work there is a curiously wistful note in his attacks on the people who have escaped the pain of being alive by living in the past. Their security in a world where values seemed secure is understandable, and it is this which promotes the envy of Osborne's heroes, unable themselves to find this sense of belonging. Osborne expresses this hankering for an established order of things past amidst his virulent attacks on the order of things present:

> The intelligent political man of left wing sympathies in
> Osborne tells him—and us—that it was the faults in this
> antediluvian world which brought our world into existence,
> but the incorrigible romantic looks back admiringly, and these
> plays are the battlegrounds (hence much of the excitement)
> on which the two Osbornes fight it out.[26]

[25] *L.B.A.*, p. 68
[26] J. R. Taylor, *Anger and After*. London, 1963, p. 48.

For those who do not seek to escape the pain of being alive Osborne would seem to stipulate anger or boredom. The Sunday afternoon and evening of the Porter household stares one in the face, the only answer there, it seems, is to make tea, the never ending "cuppa" washes down their boredom. If we substitute gin or draught bass for the tea, then *The Entertainer* tells the same story. Billy is so bored that he takes long pointless walks, whilst Phoebe seeks solace in repeated visits to the cinema. Other plays establish the same atmosphere, the same claustrophobia envelops the hero. Pamela drowns herself in champagne, Laurie in whiskey and soda. The banality of life forces Bill Maitland to seek escape in numerous sordid affairs with young secretaries. Russell is prepared to sacrifice his freedom for his newly found riches, undaunted by his deadening prospects. A fate which awaits not only the blood royal but the blood Dillon, George preferring to bury himself in the family life of the Elliots, and thus, like the others, escape the pain of creative existence.

To Osborne life without a worthy set of values can only be one of boredom, concerned as it is with needless trivia. Thus he is prepared to expose cruelly the petty ends of the mini-mind. Bill Maitland mouths Osborne's view of the masses. Maitland, a man at the end of his tether, is not concerned with the niceties of society and contemptuously describes the "man in the street":

> BILL. You know who they are? . . . They're the ones who go out on Bank Holiday in the car! And have mascots in the rear window.

Proud of his wit, he goes on:

> BILL. They are the people who go up on every year like it was Holy Communion to have a look at the Christmas decorations in Regent Street.[27]

This seems a peculiarly negative position for Osborne to adopt, for he is, in essence, a positive writer, and even here, with this blatant condemnation of the masses, and his despair at their lack of fight, there is still the suggestion of something better if only people would join the crusade. Osborne's attitude and his

---

[27] *I.E.*, pp. 24-5.

words seem both critical and negative but they are, in fact, a demand for a degree of response and care beyond that which is apparent at the moment. Osborne's anger is positive, it is the outward manifestation of his dissatisfaction with the world as it stands. He refuses to stand by and see opportunities for creative and imaginative life diminished and constricted. Osborne will not accept isolation. This is a positive attitude. What he wishes to do is to expose those things to which he objects and to promote those things which he believes valuable to uphold. To that end his themes are directed; he uses plot, characters, and language, torrents of language, to establish and maintain his fundamental belief. His belief that man is good and simply needs to be freed to be himself. In this belief lies Osborne's artistic integrity—his creative spark is lit by this emotion.

VIII

Language

By his use of language John Osborne attempts to penetrate our indifference, and to make us care about the way in which we live. He questions the values by which we guide ourselves. If these values seem somewhat tarnished today that is all the more reason for us to *concern* ourselves about them. Even if we take exception to some of his ideas or statements, we cannot deny the quality of the language used to voice them for he has a way of making his characters speak so that we never question their words. If we criticise anything, it is the idea expressed, never the expression. We already know the impact his plays had, and much of this was due to the fact that Osborne captured the imagination of a generation in search of a leader. With his vivid statements he became the spokesman for that generation, voicing its opinions. The voice he used was authentic. It possessed the tenor of those years. It was disbelieving, clever, uninhibited. There was no place in it for the ornate or delicate. The public came to listen to that voice, for it mirrored their own confusion, and at the same time it gave an expression to their dissatisfaction with the injustices of the period.

Osborne's plays expressed the despair of a frustrated idealism. They did so in a language which was new to the theatre—everyday English. A vocabulary which could be heard in the street, in shops, at football matches, in the cinema, and in the home. *Look Back in Anger* brought contemporary language to the stage, a point just as important in terms of "the breakthrough" as any other, and a fact which Osborne acknowledges himself:

> . . . one can find different ways of breaking out without using different stages. Although *Look Back in Anger* was a formal,

rather old fashioned play, I think that it broke out by its use of language. . . .[1]

Society is diminished. Can it be saved? "Yes", says Osborne, "if it can be woken up". Language was to be the "pep-pill". Jimmy Porter was much more real with his use of the idioms of his age than he would have been had Osborne used the literary style of the plays of an earlier period. Osborne was not concerned with fashion for not only did he draw upon a vocabulary made up of normal everyday words, he also gave his principal characters long monologues to deliver. He does not approve of these speeches being called monologues which he thinks is a rather scornful term. These speeches work theatrically and dramatically. They work because he *arranges* them to do so. The "small change" dialogue is equally effective, and we need to acknowledge his mastery of both forms—monologue and dialogue. Naturally the long speeches impress us more, for in them we hear the articulate flow of Osborne's ideas achieving their lyric effect, and ordinary everyday phrases and words take on new meaning. The action of the plays never completely stops during one of these vast speeches and their wit and humour keep the plays alive and buoyant. If society is to be saved, it is by these monologues that it will be prompted into action and the significance of our condition realised.

If we think of that long speech in *Inadmissible Evidence* where Bill Maitland, realising he has lost grip on life, desperately tries to cling to his daughter's affection, we can appreciate the full effect of Osborne's mastery of language. Bill knows deep inside himself that he has already lost her, yet he still tries to impart some parental advice. Unwittingly he sentimentalises his own dreams of youth, and manages to alienate his daughter even more, by attacking her "society". We clearly see Osborne's "alternative set of values". Bill's daughter, Jane, stands silent and expressionless throughout the whole performance. It begins in full flood, with Bill angry that people no longer hide the fact that they are ignoring him, and continues as Bill dreams of how he would have liked things to be. There are subtle

[1] "That Awful Museum", John Osborne interview with R. Findlater. *Twentieth Century*, February 1961.

pauses and transitions throughout, and when Bill finally fails
at the end, it is because his longing was too great.

BILL. They're all pretending to ignore me. No they're not
pretending, they are! And that'll be the going of you except
that it's happened already. Of course, it has, ages ago.
Look at me. Why you can't have looked at me and seen
anything, what, not for years, not since you were a little tiny
girl and I used to take you out and hold your hand in the
street. I always used to think then that when you're the
age you are now, I'd take you out to restaurants for dinner,
big restaurants like I used to think posh restaurants were
like, with marble columns and glass and orchestras. . . .
Do you want to get rid of me? Do *you*? Um? Because I
want to get rid of you . . . the reason for that is because I
know: That when I see you, I cause you little else but distaste
or distress, or, at the least, your own vintage, swinging,
indifference. But nothing, certainly not your swinging
distaste can match what I feel for you. Or any of those who
are more and more like you. I hear what you say, the sounds
you make, the few jokes you make, the wounds you inflict
without even longing to hurt, there is no lather or fear in you,
all cool, dreamy, young, cool and not a proper blemish,
forthright, unimpressed, contemptuous of ambition but good
and pushy all the same. . . . And you dance with each other,
in such a way I would never have been able to master. But,
and this is the but, I still don't think what you're doing will
ever, even, even, even, even approach the fibbing, mumping,
pinched little worm of energy eating away in this me, of
mine, I mean. That is: which is that of being slowly munched
and then diminished together . . . if you should one day start
to shrink slowly into an unremarkable, gummy little whole
into a world outside the care and consciousness of anyone,
you'll have no rattlings of shame or death, there'll be no little
sweating, eruptions of blood, no fevers or clots of flesh
splitting anywhere or haemorrhage. You'll have done
everything well and sensibly and stylishly. You'll know it
wasn't worth a candle that ever burned. You will have to
be blown out, snuffed, decently, and not watched spluttering
and spilling and hardening. You know what God is supposed
to have said, well in Sunday School, anyway? God said,
He said: "Be fruitful and multiply and replenish the earth.
And *subdue* it. It seems to me Jane, little Jane, you don't

look little any longer, you are on your way at last, all, to doing all four of them. For the first time. Go on now.[2]

This "speech" ranges through a whole stream of consciousness, and, in effect, through a whole lifetime. Maitland's hopes and aspirations, his indignities and his defeat, are there. So is his warning to us all. He hopes that his daughter will realise the truth before he did. Despairing that his life might have been spent in vain, he attacks Jane:

> BILL. Do you want to get rid of me? Do you? Um? Because I want to get rid of you.

Then a pause, and gathering himself, he coolly regains control of his emotions and the situation, telling his daughter she can't leave; but then Bill loses this mastery by trying to justify himself. He analyses Jane's generation, yet in his jealousy and final flare of defiance we know that he has lost the battle—for neither his daughter, nor anyone else will listen to what he has to say. He passes on to Jane his grip on life. Knowing that he has certainly lost control, the speech has slowed up, the pauses have become more deliberate, the tone more resigned. His speech has ranged from tenderness to cold fury, yet throughout, it is full of common ordinary words and phrases. Topical modern idioms abound "swinging indifference", "good and pushy", "your young noises", "you kink your innocent way along", all of them direct from normal daily existence. But the effect is much more than that of overheard conversation, or of a page read from a book. Bill's words have star quality, they are "larger than life". This is not due to the length of the speech or even its content, but to its organisation. That means to say the way in which the words and sentences are arranged, and how changes of speed and mood are achieved. In this rambling speech we see the real importance of timing.

What is true for this speech of Maitland's is equally valid for those of other Osborne characters. Were we to examine other examples our conclusions would be substantially the same, even though the particularities would be different. Similarly all the principal characters so dominate their "play"

[2] *I.E.*, pp. 102-7.

that the minor characters are more or less "straight-men", feeding punch lines to the "heroes". Only occasionally do other people have a chance to stand and speak for themselves. Ruth does in *Epitaph for George Dillon,* and the Colonel and the Knight are allowed some questions in *Look Back in Anger* and *Luther* respectively, as is Constance in *Time Present,* but this is about the sum of it.

When we speak of dialogue we must distinguish between that involving the central figure and that between other characters. There is little of the latter, and much of the former is really monologue interrupted by a "holding" remark from somebody else. This is even true of his group play, *The Hotel in Amsterdam,* where Laurie immediately dominates the conversation drawing in and shutting out the others as he wishes. To some extent Osborne weakens all his plays by failing to give depth to the minor characters. Yet this seems deliberate, for his intention is to create vibrant powerful lead parts, and to do this there must necessarily be some sacrifice. His heroes communicate with the audience directly through the mouthpiece monologues, rather than through any interplay with the other characters who are never allowed to exist at the same level of emotional appreciation as the heroes.

It is the stark rhetoric of his principal characters which captures our imagination, and Osborne renders this theatrical language perfectly. Tynan pertinently noted that:

> . . . poet and dialectician he may not be, but master of rhetoric he assuredly is. . . . He has raised fair ground barking to the level and intensity of art.[3]

Osborne's words are blunt, but strung together they gain an exaggerated histrionic force which is disturbingly real. His writing is provocatively honest. He is a master of repetition, using this to hammer home his points. This is not necessarily a weakness, for real conversation is certainly repetitive. There are remarkable patterns of reiteration and inversion to be found in any analysis of actual conversation. What Osborne did was to translate these half-phrases and abrupt transitions, the constant repetition and patterns of common speech, into

---

[3] *The Observer,* 30 Jul. 1961.

rhetorical power. Jimmy Porter works great energy into his scorn for Alison's mother:

> JIMMY. That old bitch should be dead! Well? Aren't I right? I said she's an old bitch, and should be dead! What's the matter with you? Why don't you leap to her defence?
> CLIFF. Jimmy don't!
> JIMMY. If someone said something like that about me, she'd react soon enough—she'd spring into her well known lethargy, and say nothing! I say she ought to be dead![4]

This is a good illustration of reiteration and of rhetoric, the fill-in—"Jimmy don't"—is brushed aside by a Jimmy anxious to get on with his tirade, and his words fill the air. It is in the speaker's state of feeling that the true impact, the real anger lies, rather than in what is said. Osborne's plays are a kind of vocal self-analysis in which his characters explore the nature of their own existence. In doing so they question the value of the environment they inhabit. Should they feel that there is some injustice or evil to be exposed then they will do so repeatedly until we *must* be aware of it. The only thing you can do with a principle is to repeat it. Napoleon's words "la répétition est la plus forte des figures de rhétorique" are very appropriate.

Certainly Osborne lashes out if he thinks it necessary, but in doing so he ensures that his language is full of imaginative life. When something is evil he makes it sound evil. Martin Luther's condemnation of the papal bull illustrates this impetuous hyperbolic force:

> LUTHER. I have been served with a piece of paper. Let me tell you about it. It has come to me from a latrine called Rome, that capital of the devil's own sweet empire. It is called the papal bull and claims to excommunicate me, Dr Martin Luther. These lies they rise up from paper like fumes from the bog of Europe; because papal decretals are the devil's excretals. I'll hold it up for you to see properly. You see the signature? Signed beneath the seal of the Fisherman's Ring by one certain midden cock called Leo, an overindulged jakes attendant to Satan himself, a glittering worm in excrement, known to you as his holiness the Pope.

[4] *L.B.A.*, p. 53.

You may know him as the head of the Church. Which he may still be: like a fish is the head of a cat's dinner: eyes without sight clutched to a stick of sucked bones. God has told me: there can be no dealings between this cat's dinner and me.[5]

Whilst this harangue comes from one of Osborne's historical plays it is very similar in tone and conception to George Dillon's epistle against Mr and Mrs Elliot in *Epitaph for George Dillon*, where he describes their wedding photograph:

GEORGE. Look at the wedding group. Look at it. It's like a million other grisly groups—all tinted in unbelievable pastels; round shouldered girls with crinkled-up hair, open mouths, and bad teeth. The bridegroom looks as gormless as he's feeling lecherous, and the bride—the bride's looking as though she's just been thrown out of an orgy at a druids reunion. Mr and Mrs Elliot at their wedding. It stands there like a comic monument to the macabre farce that has gone on between them in this house ever since that greatest day in a girl's life thirty-five years ago.[6]

Pamela, Osborne's sole heroine, voices her opinions in the same tone as Osborne's heroes, and we cannot mistake the disgust so often present in their words:

PAMELA. You should beware of lady writers. They hover and dart about like preying fish in a tank. They've their eyes on you and little tape recorders whining away behind their ears by way of breathing apparatus. Then they swallow you up whole and spew you up later, dead and distorted. Nothing has happened to you in the meantime except that they turn you into waste material. Because the trouble with lady writers is they've usually no digestive juices. They're often even surprised you're not pleased. There, I gobbled you up whole. Aren't I swift, don't I move, don't I watch. Like hell you do. You just can't deal with it decently once you've got it.[7]

This is in almost exactly the same tone as Jimmy Porter's condemnation of Brother Nigel, and it carries a similar element of warning in it.

As we build up a picture of the Osborne "heroes", by

[5] *L.*, p. 79.   [6] *E.G.D.*, p. 59.   [7] *T.P.*, p. 58.

reference to their monologues, we see that they use the same words, the same colloquial phrases and idioms. Mary McCarthy acknowledged this in her controversial article "Verdict on Osborne", in which she drew together several of the points we have made:

> Kipling's advice to a writer was: "Don't do what you *can* do: do what you can't! . . . Kipling's advice is useful, if taken in moderation. Any writer who follows it will not commit the fault of repeating himself or fall into self-plagiarism. Everyone is prone to this fault, and particularly a writer with a distinctive "voice" like Osborne. Such a writer, like a coloratura or a counter-tenor, finds that he is limited to parts of experience, as it were, already written for his voice's range and timbre. He writes by ear, listening anxiously for the musical cue that will give him his pitch. . . . At the same time such a writer must get tired of hearing the sound of his own voice, just as the hero of "Inadmissible Evidence", who is always on the witness stand, testifying, gets tired of hearing himself. . . . Reiteration is the basic mode of the Osborne harangue and repetition is the basic plot of the Osborne plays: the last-act curtain rises on a new girl at the ironing-board and everything will start over again.[8]

To be dramatic, words must be put together and expressed with feeling, the state of feeling from which they stem will determine the voice with which they are uttered. Osborne's voice was that of a man bellowing with rage at being trapped into a pattern of existence from which, however desperately he wishes to escape, he cannot. John Osborne fights desperately and loudly for what he believes to be right. There is no need for subtlety—the quiet and clever will not be heard on the battleground of today, perhaps the loud, strident, and insistent will.

We have discussed with reference to some lengthy quotation how Osborne uses language, now we must ask ourselves what that language consists of. Kenneth Tynan mentioned in an aside to his review of *Epitaph for George Dillon*, that a good subject for a thesis would be an estimation of the influence on Mr Osborne's later plays of *The Vortex* and *Red Peppers*, bearing in mind that the dismissive use of "little", favoured by Mr

---

[8] *The Observer*, 4 Jul. 1965.

Osborne in a plethora of phrases beginning "nasty little", "sordid little", etc. . . . was pioneered by Noel Coward in the twenties. If Mr Tynan would care to know the number of times the word "little" occurs throughout Osborne's plays, it is 353. The fondness for the adjective "little" is only one of Osborne's preferences. The word "old" appears 355 times, and like "little" it is used in a pejorative sense as well as in its more literal sense such as in "piffing little success", or "poor old Bennet". Both of these words are frequently used in combination with others, often proper names and nouns, such as "Old Charlie Rowse", "Poor old Mum", and with other adjectives when they form insults, "he's an ugly little devil". Insult is an Osborne speciality, and another word, "poor", joins "little" and "old" in most of these expressions, one common insult being "you poor bastard". Osborne's most usual expletives are "bloody", "bastard", and various combinations of "damn". Any play will give ample evidence. *Luther*, for example, with its description of beer as "damned monk's piss", or of Martin himself, as a "double faced German bastard". Yet Osborne does not confine himself to only three expletives, and other common words join bloody, damn, and bastard, in most of his curses—"you bloody right wing old poup", or, "I said you bloody wait, you horrible little skivvy". He is also particularly fond of phrases such as "Good Heavens!" "Oh, my God!" "God-forsaken place!" "Like Hell!" "What the devil!" Almost 200 of them are to be found in the plays. One word which occurs very frequently in the "contemporary" plays, but hardly at all elsewhere, is "bit", which is synonymous with "little", as in "a bit odd". It is, in fact, the third most frequent word (excluding the common prepositions, conjunctions, pronouns, etc. . . .). One notices that these words are often found in common everyday speech, and it is indeed quite rare to find any "sophisticated" vocabulary in Osborne's work. If he does use a word which might cause any problem to the "man in the street" he takes care to give a full explanation. When Jimmy Porter finds an adjective applicable to his wife he defines it for his audience:

> JIMMY. Pusillanimous. Adjective. Wanting of firmness of
> mind, of small courage, having a little mind, mean spirited,

cowardly; timid of mind. From the Latin pusillus, very little, and animus the mind.[9]

If a "high-brow" word is used, not only is it explained, but the definition usually contains some implied criticism of those who use it:

> GEORGE. It's rather like calling bad breath "halitosis" don't you think?[10]

As if to emphasise the "ordinariness" of his vocabulary, Osborne employs a substantial number of slang words and phrases. He integrates these into the dialogue to add some kind of sinewy strength. These expressions are usually used in short expletive bursts. In every play there are examples: "who went bonkers"; "a lot of wogs"; "every tart and pansy boy"; "we are going posh"; "the big old gob"; "niffy dormouse"; "gives me the creeps"—the list is inexhaustible.

We have said a great deal about the naturalness of Osborne's vocabulary, but the real imaginative force behind his language is primarily due to its imagery. His characters rarely grope for words or parallels with which to express themselves. The components of this imagery may well be ordinary everyday words, but the word pictures are never commonplace. George Dillon expresses this feeling of having one's words on the tip of the tongue, when he compares himself to Josie. At the same time he effectively distinguishes between Osborne's heroes and their pedantic straight-men.

> GEORGE. I have a mind and feelings that are all fingertips. Josie's mind? She can hardly spell it. And her feelings— what about them? All thumbs, thumbs that are fat and squashy—like bananas, in fact, and rather sickly.[11]

It is with this imaginative feeling and fingertip control that Osborne builds his vibrant arresting imagery.

In this chapter the basic problem is one of space, for it is obviously impossible to provide the "raw material" on which we base our conclusions. We could use some form of numerical analysis and say that with reference to the theme of anger, the play, *Look Back in Anger*, contains 45 metaphors (excluding

[9] *L.B.A.*, p. 22. [10] *E.G.D.*, p. 44. [11] *Op. cit.*, p. 59.

hyperbole), whilst *The Entertainer* has 53, and *Inadmissible Evidence* only 24. Alternatively, we could discuss each play in turn, and note for example, that in *Epitaph for George Dillon* there are 10 similes relating to anger, only five to class, and but four to despair. Both methods, when we remember that there are several forms of imagery, many themes, and 13 plays, are of course impractical. We must trust therefore that our assumptions regarding language will be accepted as provable, and that the examples which are given will be taken as representative of the facts which would be that proof.

Characteristically Osborne bases much of his imagery on the spectre of war or the hunt. The vocabulary of battle is constantly before us: kill, death, butcher, beat, destroy, enemy, slaughter, murder, agony, trap, snare, wound, stab, rage. Incredibly, the list builds up. In the most ordinary of situations the imagery constantly takes on this appearance:

> LAURIE. Someone always wants to be useful or flattered or gulled or just plain whipped to death or cast out into the knackers yard by King Sham. Well let him go ahead and get himself crucified this time. I know him not.[12]

or later in the same play:

> LAURIE. She feels invaded, distorted. About to be destroyed.[13]

Both of these examples are taken from non-violent scenes, yet the "dingy assault course" is still present. In the more obvious attacks we hardly find a line without some reference to the constant battle Osborne fights.

Many figures of speech come from historical sources which is another of Osborne's preferences. This is particularly true of the "contemporary plays", and similes are especially subject to this treatment:

> JIMMY. A simple visit to the lavatory sounded like a medieval siege.[14]

George Dillon combines both war imagery and historical analogy when he protests against the audiences he has played to:

> GEORGE. I've got to fight almost everyone of those people in the auditorium. Right from the stalls to the gallery, to

[12] *H.A.*, p. 94.   [13] *Op. cit.*, p. 120.   [14] *L.B.A.*, p. 25.

the Vestal Virgins in the boxes! My God, it's a gladiatoria
combat! Me against them! Me and Mighty Them![15]

When the playwright wishes to gain our sympathy for a character
he invariably uses imagery which refers to animals. The bears
and squirrels of the Porters immediately spring to mind, but
the technique is much in evidence elsewhere. The most
obvious example of this is provided by the scene in *The Hotel
in Amsterdam* where Laurie ascribes an animal personality to
each of his companions:

> LAURIE. You can't be loving friends with a dinosaur.
> ANNIE. What are you then?
> LAURIE. A mouse—what else!
> ANNIE. Some mouse. With the soul of a tiger.
> LAURIE. A mouse. With the soul of a toothless bear.
> ANNIE. What's Gus?
> LAURIE. Gus? He's a walking, talking, living dolphin.
> ANNIE. Amy?
> LAURIE. An un-neurotic fallow-deer.
> ANNIE. And Dan?
> LAURIE. Dan, he's a bit difficult. Rather cool, absent-
> minded but observant. Orang-utan.[16]

And so it goes on, an extended imaginative game giving us a
delicate insight into the characters' essential natures. In the
play *Luther*, the "animal" imagery is used to give a really vivid
expression to Martin's agony, both physical and spiritual, as he
contemplates the nature of faith:

> MARTIN. .... And seated there, my head down, on that privy
> just as when I was a little boy, I couldn't reach down to my
> breath for the sickness in my bowels, as I seemed to sense
> beneath a large rat, a heavy, wet, plague rat, slashing at
> my privates with its death's teeth.[17]

This is very emotive, for we shrink inside ourselves at the thought
of the rat's slashing teeth.

The metaphor is the predominant Osborne image, certainly
if one includes the more forceful hyperbole. They outnumber
all other images in the ratio of $2:1$. The only other figure of
speech commonly found is the simile. There is some personifi-

[15] *E.G.D.*, p. 56.   [16] *H.A.*, pp. 109-10.   [17] *L.*, p. 63.

cation, several euphemisms, but hardly any litotes, synecdoches, or metonymies.

Metaphors give effect and vitality to the long speeches of the central characters, they are used to bring colour to well-constructed line-drawings. It is part of Osborne's talent that they never jar or obtrude, but take their place within the flow of speech, adding light and shade to the effect. These metaphors are never decorative, they are organic and express a complex of thought and feeling which is so subtle and precise that it could not be expressed in any other way. George Holyoake, the blasphemer of *A Subject of Scandal and Concern* uses an extended metaphor to show how society has always obstructed innovation:

> HOLYOAKE. What threats there were of Hell and flames, what splashing about of fire and brimstones, what judgement on these men choked with their beefsteak on a Friday. Such frying, such barbecuing and everyone dripping in a flood of sin and gravy and not the smallest notion of a red herring anyway.[18]

This provides full expression to the idea of religious intolerance and concern over incidentals; and note how Osborne has introduced the "red herring" pun into the last sentence to add effect. These extended metaphors are evocative and full of meaning. They give curious insight into the character of the speaker for they usually uncover secret fears.

We can, however, leave aside contexts and still appreciate the aptness of Osborne's imagery. Jimmy Porter describes "poor old Daddy" as:

> JIMMY. Just one of those sturdy plants left over from Edwardian wilderness that can't understand why the sun isn't shining any more.[19]

We do not need to know anything about the situation which prompted this remark, for the image has the strength of descriptiveness to stand by itself. In the same way we know Paul Slickey when his wife describes him:

> LESLEY. There is a constant stain of endeavour underneath his emotional armpits. It throws off quite an unpleasant smell of sour ideals.[20]

[18] *S.S.C.*, p. 33.   [19] *L.B.A.*, p. 66.   [20] *W.P.S.*, p. 50.

We learn also something of the character who utters these words, the cold, efficient, business-like Lesley.

It is interesting to see, that in those plays which are generally regarded to have been Osborne's less successful, *The World of Paul Slickey*, *The Blood of the Bambergs*, *Under Plain Cover*, and *A Subject of Scandal and Concern*, imagery is very much less frequent. We might, with some justification, attribute the success of the "public" plays to Osborne's mastery of imagery. It is to these plays that we must restrict ourselves if we wish to see the really colourful Osborne metaphor, to appreciate, for example, the lyric imagery of *Luther*:

> MARTIN. They're trying to turn me into a fixed star, Father, but I'm a shifting planet.[21]
>
> I was fighting a bear in a garden without flowers.[22]

Martin, surrounded by physical trivia in his search for spiritual redemption, has the command of language to render this battle:

> MARTIN. I awoke in my cell, all soaking in the devil's bath.[23]

Another historical play, *A Patriot for Me*, contains numerous examples of the short abusive metaphor Osborne constructs so well: "you Jewish prig, you whitened sepulchre", "you old temple built on a sewer", "you little painted toy, you puppet"; and in the final harangue of Redl against the Spanish, there is one particularly fine metaphor:

> REDL. . . . damned Spaniards . . . inventing bridal lace to line coffins with. They stink of death.[24]

The majority of hostile images however are to be found in the contemporary plays where they reveal something of the character of the speaker, for we relish the words chosen, and the vehemence or despair with which the heroes voice their feelings. Jimmy Porter ranges from white-hot anger to abject despair and frustration, and his feelings are perfectly rendered in the metaphor:

> JIMMY. I want to stand up in your tears and splash about in them and sing.[25]

[21] *L.*, p. 99.   [22] *Op. cit.*, p. 10.   [23] *Op. cit.*, p. 20.
[24] *P.M.*, p. 122.   [25] *L.B.A.*, p. 59.

George voices his disillusionment in *Epitaph for George Dillon* with:

> GEORGE. Always put the gun in the other man's hand. That's my rule of life.[26]

And he can be just as incredulous as Jimmy:

> GEORGE. Norah doesn't even exist—she's just a hole in the air.[27]

Osborne uses the metaphor to add colour and weight to his plea for a more worthy attitude to life. He constantly rails out against those who hem in our natural expression:

> LAURIE. He takes nothing out of the air round *his* head. Only us. Insinuates his grit into all the available oysters. And if ever any tiny pearls should appear from those tight, invaded creatures, he whips off with them, appropriates them and strings them together for his own necklace.[28]

Yet even with cynicism such as Laurie's, Osborne's characters still care. Archie Rice is not, as he tries to pretend ". . . dead behind the eyes". Neither has Bill Maitland given up hope, for his critical remarks about others give evidence of this. When he tells his secretary, Joy, his feelings about the "languid pipe cleaner of an accountant" she is engaged to, he is in fact warning her against the "Promised Land" he stunningly mocks elsewhere: "Jones entering the Promised Land in his mini". Bill is warning us all not to become the "flatulent, purblind, mating weasels", he thinks block the land from one end to the other.

These are metaphors of "idea", and however disturbing they may be, they reflect the world of today and its attitudes, rather than that of yesterday. They are always interesting and vigorous. They may be full of surprise, but their vivid descriptiveness illuminates Osborne's values and ideals. We can say with Leonido, that because of them, "My ears are not overgrown with old man's moss".

Simile plays its part in this battle and Osborne's similes

[26] *E.G.D.*, p. 64.   [27] *Op. cit.*, p. 60.   [28] *H.A.*, p. 117.

spurt from the mouth even more rapidly than do his metaphors. Most of them are derogatory:

> PAMELA. No wonder she's so solemn! Why she's got tits like old ski-socks filled with sand.[29]

But there are also emotional similes to be found which heighten the sense of insecurity and isolation of the central characters, such as Laurie's tentative attempt to reassure himself by asking:

> LAURIE. Do you ever have a little lace curtain in front of your eyes? Like little spermy tadpoles paddling across your eyeballs?[30]

Luther contains more similes than any other Osborne play, and they are frequently used to describe Martin's physical ailments, both his constipation and his continual perspiration. Some rise to poetic lyrism, as when Luther pleads with God to instill in him the faith and knowledge he so desperately needs:

> MARTIN. Breathe into me, like a lion into the mouth of a stillborn cub.[31]

As with the metaphors, Osborne's similes are drawn from certain common sources, history and war amongst them. Jimmy Porter sentimentally recalls his ex-girl friend Madeleine with the words:

> JIMMY. To sit on top of a bus with her was like setting out with Ulysses.[32]

In these terms Madeleine is contrasted to Alison, Jimmy's pedantic wife. In another evocative and very sensitive image, Bill Maitland describes his state of feelings:

> BILL. . . . all I feel is as if my head were bigger and falling off, like a mace.[33]

This is extremely arresting and we can immediately focus upon this symbol, as we can when George Dillon admits to his own state of feeling with the words:

> GEORGE. At this moment I feel about as empty and as thread-bare as my pockets.[34]

[29] *T.P.*, p. 32. [30] *H.A.*, p. 102. [31] *L.*, p. 80.
[32] *L.B.A.*, p. 19. [33] *I.E.*, p. 35. [34] *E.G.D.*, p. 56.

Osborne chooses readily recognisable parallels for us, his imagery never demands prior knowledge in the way that, for example, T. S. Eliot's, does. There is nothing abstruse or *recherché* about it. It is used to arrest, and for language to achieve that effect in the theatre, as Osborne's does, even out of context, is a mark of significant success. Of course, brash strident exaggerated hyperbole will always shock, and will inevitably batter audiences into some kind of receptiveness: but Osborne's imagery does more than that. Its compressiveness is provoking and its power is clear for all to see, yet we should remember that much of it is also tender and lyrical. It is used emotionally and descriptively, to heighten our sense of what is happening, to straighten our appreciation of the situation, to let us understand the foibles of character more easily, and above all, to quicken our interest.

Another feature worth mentioning is the way in which Osborne "plays" with words, for he seems to enjoy their manipulation and invention. We see this everywhere, from the coupling of "Annie-Laurie" in *The Hotel in Amsterdam*, to that play's "fanfuckingtastik", and *Inadmissible Evidence's* "vote-wheedling catch-fart", or *Time Present's* "clever dickdyke's thirty bob's worth". In *A Bond Honoured* we get the following play on words:

> TIZON. Now that she's to be a bride—
> LEONIDO. Not may or may not have. Has. Did. Is. Not was, might may. Is. Well?[35]

And later:

> GERARDO. Bell. Wedding bell?
> LEONIDO. Bedding well. Yes.[36]

Here, a pleonasm is used to gain rhetorical emphasis. A similar pattern is to be found in *Luther*; Martin has just been received into the Order and his father Hans turns to Lucas:

> HANS. . . . what do you think?
> LUCAS. Think of what?
> HANS. Yes, think man, think, what do you think, pen and ink, think of all that?[37]

[35] *B.H.*, p. 18.   [36] *Op. cit.*, p. 27.   [37] *L.*, pp. 14-15.

This is a good example of repetition, and rhyming slang, in addition to showing Osborne's delight in original and amusing constructions.

He has a marked quirk for creating "funny" names. In *Epitaph for George Dillon* we see several: "George what's-his-name"; "Georgie Porgie-puddeny-pie"; Mr Colwyn-pussy-Stuart; Mr Colwyn-phoney-Stuart. *The Entertainer* is the most fertile field, with Sir Somebody Pearson; Mr Graham Thing; and the oft-repeated "Captain Charlie Double-back-Action-hyphen-breech loading Gore of Elm Lodge, Shrewskesbury, Glos". Proper names are humorously treated in other plays. In *The World of Paul Slickey* characters masquerade under the names of Father Evilgreene, Mrs Giltedge-Whyte, and Teddy Maroon. The name Wilhelm is toyed with in *The Blood of the Bambergs*:

> WIMPLE. Princess Wilhelm or, as I think we might venture to call him, as they all seem to do, at least in this part of the country, our Prince Will. Our Prince Will will—Wilhelm will—be the first royal bridegroom. . . .[38]

From these examples we see how Osborne extracts humour from his love of language by means of unusual arrangements or by emphasising a particular word or phrase. There is, of course, a much stronger current of humour permeating his plays than this particular type. His language is so direct and open that there can never be any doubt in one's mind what is meant, there are no hidden jibes, his criticism is plain and direct. To make these attacks more acceptable Osborne wraps many of them in humour, he makes us laugh as a relief, yet we still appreciate the meaning. Of course, these jokes do not work as well on the written page as they do in the theatre, for they need the living response of an audience.

Our final remark about Osborne's language is to stress how *real* it is. By using the colloquial idioms, clichés, and words of everyday life, he creates a language which is disturbing in its likeness to our own speech. The self-discovery of his characters is also our own discovery.

The very nature of his subject matter makes it inevitable

[38] *B.B.*, p. 15.

that he shocks some people by the language he uses, and by doing so, Osborne has helped push back the conventional boundaries of what plays are about. That in itself is a valuable contribution to the theatre.

Osborne has always cared very much for what he has to say —he is in that sense a teacher. However, he is equally concerned with how to say it—for the expression will determine the reception of his ideas. Thus his language is direct, open, and forceful. He is concerned with "how to say it", but not with "how to say it nicely". He has in fact created a new tone of voice in the theatre, one which is entirely his own, and one which is always recognisable as such.

IX

Appreciation

*You hear me Ronnie? You've got to care, you've got
to care or you'll die.*[1]

A PLAY has a meaning and a separate artistic entity. It
both *means* and *is*. When we go to the theatre, we, the
audience, are really trying to look at life through the eyes
of someone else. We wish to broaden our experience, to
be aware of emotions other than our own. It is impossible to
admit audiences to experiences, to give them emotional
"shivers", unless those experiences are part of a pattern which
has been previously established, for the ideas and situations
common to an age contribute to the life of a play. Drama
conveys an experience and tells truths about it which must be
based on a realistic interpretation of the conditions.

John Osborne's plays obey this dictum, they can be regarded
as moments of spirit. He is not a didactic writer in the accepted
sense, for the speech of his characters comes from within the
plays, it never interrupts or disturbs. The *something said* and
the *something made* are inextricably blended. Stripped to the
barest essentials his plays are no more than their heroes, who,
caring for life, try to save humanity from a sea of meaningless-
ness. This is not to say that Osborne disregards the other
elements of drama, but rather, that these elements are overshadowed by that "excess of humanity" symbolised in the heroes.

Drama consists fundamentally of plot, character, dialogue,
thought, and enactment. With the last of these we are not
concerned in this book, although in passing we might add that
Osborne has been well served by his actors, as indeed they have
by him. His plays perform well, plot and dialogue giving
body to character and theme.

Osborne is commonly regarded as an innovator, but this is

[1] Arnold Wesker, *Chicken Soup with Barley*.

hardly true as far as his plots are concerned. The raw material of plot is life, not average daily life in all its banality, but rather its extreme climaxes or hidden forms. Whilst emotion is obviously present in real life, it is much more present in drama. To see drama in something is to perceive conflict, and the art of drama must take note of the mishaps and disasters of ordinary life for it is in them that conflict is revealed. Osborne's drama is full of conflict, generated by the inflexibility of both society and his characters. He is fully aware of the umbilical connexion between art and life, and his theatrical expression is based deep in human nature.

There are many kinds of plots, ranging from "unified" to "episodic" and Osborne uses most of them. *A Patriot for Me*, for example, has a definite climax with Redl's suicide, whilst *Inadmissible Evidence* just stops in mid-stream, its climax in effect is the opening nightmare scene. Other plays fit somewhere in between. *Look Back in Anger* would appear to reach its climax when Alison returns to seek acceptance, but then the play goes on to show the reconciled couple's flight into an imaginary world of bears and squirrels, leaving us with a taste of their future boredom. *Luther* is the most episodic in sequence of Osborne's plays, and parallels the style of Brecht's *Galileo*. Some attempt is made to present the monk, Luther, in an equivocal light. The first two acts are sympathetic portrayals of his earlier conflicts of conscience and the effective vigour of his attack on a corrupt Church, whilst the third act shows his dismissal of the peasants' rebellion which he himself helped to foster. Osborne's last play, *The Hotel in Amsterdam*, has virtually no plot at all, concentrating on the conversation of the characters to animate it until the very last page.

Osborne has never whole-heartedly adopted a Brechtian technique for his plots, for Brecht was seeking a detached and objective approach by the use of his "*verfremdung*" effect, whilst Osborne uses it to *increase* our emotional awareness. *The Entertainer* seems Brechtian in structure, with Archie Rice's routines commenting on the action of the realistic inner play: but whilst these jokes and songs are symbolic and comment made in them has universality, what they actually do is to involve us even more with Archie. When we see him on stage, when we listen to his pathetically unfunny jokes, we know him better, we accept him back into the family story more sympathetically—the alienation effect is reversed. Osborne is only Brechtian in the sense that he wants his spectator to be an active and not passive member of society. Where Brecht believed that the best form of play to encourage detached rational observation was the epic narrative, with its loose sequence of scenes, Osborne believes that unity can only be given to this sequence by an emotional concentration on one character. Brecht discounted this hero worship and even questioned the value of an absolute standard of ethics. Central characters were presented ambiguously, as in the dialectical treatment of Galileo's recantation. When Osborne chooses to address his audience directly he does so, not by technique, but by characterisation, he seeks emotional response first, only later does thinking play its part.

The content of a play is more important to Osborne than its form. He readily admits that any innovation made by *Look Back in Anger* was due not to its plot or structure, but to its subject matter and language. All his plays, even those tackling historical subjects, reveal truths about life as we know it, presented in easily comprehensible fashion. Osborne's attachment to the episodic form is due less to Brecht's influence, than to the greater scope and freedom it affords.

British audiences appreciate opinion more than art anyway, and public taste notices Osborne's muddled general attacks much more than it does his undoubted theatrical gifts. He hardly needs integrated plots for the speeches of his heroes are so fascinating in their splutterings that they rivet our attention. Osborne's is a bright compulsive theatre. Like his "heroes" he is always "having a go". Even in *The Hotel in Amsterdam* where Laurie epitomises the disenchanted middle-aged, Osborne still allows him some "angry young" outbursts.

Osborne's first three plays possess strong situations and have effective "curtains", yet they could not be called situation drama for they are much more concerned with people than with plot. There is no real situation drama in any of Osborne's work, and even plays like *A Subject of Scandal and Concern* and *A Patriot for Me*, which imply situation drama with the hero trapped by the morality of his time, are tackled from the human viewpoint. Because of the larger than life view of the heroes, we tend to ignore the craftsman in Osborne, binding and constructing the plots around his heroes. His wide theatrical expertise is apparent if only by reason of the fact that his plays *work* in the theatre. When the technical artist is not in evidence, or when the "hero figure" is absent, then the plot fails miserably. The prime reason for these "failures" seems to be that Osborne concentrates solely on destruction and forgets everything else—hence the premature deaths of *The World of Paul Slickey*, and *The Blood of the Bambergs*.

One thing which is apparent is that Osborne's inventiveness seems to be drying up a little as far as plot is concerned. Three plays have been historical reconstructions, relying heavily on documentary sources, *A Bond Honoured*, is an adaptation of Lope de Vega's *La Fianza Satisfecha*, and the *For the Meantime* plays seem essentially to have no plot at all. In the last two, Osborne would appear to have reached the stage of admitting that his audience come to hear "his" voice, and that as long as the stage is theatrically occupied, they are happy not to question the weaknesses of individual plot constructions.

It is this identification with the self-punishing heroes which makes Osborne's work unique in the theatre today. He personifies in his heroes the condition the country is in. He is a humanist and has a humanist's feeling of responsibility, he regards his characters as instruments of change. All his plays are statements from one person to many—the many may disagree with what is expressed, but they will at least know what they are disagreeing with. Osborne's human beings are articulate, talking is their prime mode of self-assertion and self-justification. Not only are his characters articulate, they also have stamina. Rarely do real people summon up such power and vehemence. Jimmy Porter's harangue against his mother-in-law; Martin Luther's tirade against the sale of indulgences; Alfred Redl's denouncement of the Spaniards; Laurie's condemnation of K.L.; each demands the abundance of controlled energy, which, fortunately, they possess. Subject to the normal conflict of life when caught in a moment of stress the characters rant and rage at their tormentors. Through them Osborne exposes evil and injustice as he sees it, and they assert themselves and him in no unlikely manner. The content of these speeches and the action of the play must also be related to life as it exists, and it is a signal achievement of Osborne that he does this perfectly. If we remember this the criticism that his heroes "outgrow" their plays is not valid, they tower above them certainly, and their words are not limited by their context, but they are always *relevant* to that context and to similar situations.

Osborne impresses the main features of his heroes on his audiences in a most vivid manner. Each comes over complete with his own awareness of life, his own brand of rhetoric, and his own failings. Yet they share a common denominator: they are never wrong. They rarely apologise and seldom admit their faults. Society is always the culprit, never the individual. All of them are plausibly motivated and psychologically consistent, their behaviour is in keeping with their nature and their situation. In the play, *A Subject of Scandal and Concern*, the hero, George Holyoake, refuses to be baited by the officials, he stoically receives the news of his daughter's death, and not for one moment does he blame himself, right is on his side. Society, in the shape of his wife's family, is at fault, for so locked are they in their petty middle-class morality that they can stand by and watch an innocent child starve. Holyoake, determined to retain his individuality, demands from the prison chaplain that he be given a leather-bound Bible and not the standard cloth-backed edition. This is the kind of inflexibility which ensures conflict and from this drama is created. Suspense is developed by our desire to know what happens (a desire kindled by previous stimulus), and our overwhelming interest in the hero.

These heroes are emotionally alive and possess an immediacy of human response far in excess of that which society demands. Quick and intelligent to life around them, they are shattered by the lack of effort and the inertia of others. Disaster is a certain fate for they are too vital to accept the scant offerings of society. They are left to blaze away indiscriminately at the objects of their dissatisfaction, and to retreat into the oblivion of sex or drink. Even in this they find little happiness, often having to accept second best. George Dillon is representative of these

M

frustrated idealists. Blessed with "a mind and feelings which are all fingertips", he settles for the euthanasia of love and marriage to the sickly Josie Elliot. His almost neurotic determination to discover and free his talent, weakens, and George is defeated by a world he believes in his heart to have accepted the wrong values.

A common criticism claims that Osborne's characters seem so forceful that it is hard to reconcile this with their acceptance of such total defeat, but surely the individual is in a hopeless position in the face of such odds? It is the deficiency of the modern world which makes Osborne's individuals impotent. The hero's surfeit of imagination, stunned by society's lack of response or care, makes him easy prey. A much more valid criticism would be the one which claims that any "war" run on such individual lines is unlikely to be successful. Jimmy Porter, for example, pursues a class war in *Look Back in Anger* where he forces Cliff, his working-class friend, to leave, and Alison to cut herself off from her family; in other words, Jimmy rejects the working class, and makes Alison reject the upper class. To defeat Alison is probably Jimmy's revenge on her class as a whole, yet he has rejected his own as well, and the couple are left to their private world of sexual compulsion. In fairness to Osborne we should remember that the effect of his plays comes not from structure or theme, but from characterisation and language, and in this particular play the essential protest against society was made long before its downbeat ending—it was made in the very person of Jimmy Porter from the first moment we see him throw aside the Sunday newspapers in disgust.

Osborne's heroes are men at loggerheads with the inflexibility of their society. This has been a universal theme in literature. The crime of the hero and the heroine of George Orwell's 1984 was that they ignored the State and devoted themselves to each other. Lawrence's Lady Chatterley and Mellors ignored their sense of social responsibility, and they too rejected convention. In much the same way, Alfred Redl turns his back on the ethics of his society by becoming a practising homosexual. All these "relationships" make a bitter, but nonetheless necessary protest against the triviality of their times. Osborne's major interest will never be the movement of society as a whole, but rather the plight of the individual caught up in the machinations of society—the man who refuses "to be a good chap and play the game". Osborne himself is something of a "loner", for whilst he made his Atom bomb protest marches, he seems more content with scathing individual protest, as his letters to the press bear witness.

To ensure our interest in his hero figures, Osborne tends to sacrifice his minor characters, and they are never fully realised. So dominating are the principal characters, that there is very little real debate between them and the other characters. Only in two plays, *Luther* and *Epitaph for George Dillon*, is there any effective opposition to the principal. In the first, Martin expresses his opinion and position in conversations with Staupitz, Cajetan, Hans, and in dispute with Eyck. The symbolic Knight is another opponent, but the monk easily turns aside the Knight's accusations of his political motives. In the second play, the hero, George Dillon, is unable to escape from Ruth's probes, and his clash with her provides us with the meatiest of all Osborne's scenes. The term "love-hate" might well have been invented to describe their relationship:

> RUTH. George, why don't you go?
> GEORGE. Go?
> RUTH. Leave this house. Get out of here. . . .
> GEORGE. Are you serious? I haven't got a penny in the world.
> RUTH. You'll manage. You've got to. It's your only chance of survival. Am I being harsh, George? Perhaps as you say we're the same kind.
> GEORGE. That's good! Oh yes! And what about you?
> RUTH. What about me?
> GEORGE. What are you doing here? All right, you've had your go at me. But what about yourself?
> RUTH. Well?
> GEORGE. Oh, don't be so innocent, Ruth. This house! This room! This hideous, God-awful room![2]

In this exchange we see that Ruth and George are indeed the same kind of person, this in itself is a rare occurrence in a play

---

[2] *E.G.D.*, p. 58.

by Osborne, for usually only the hero has the right of attack. So charged with emotion is the interplay between the two and so engrossed are we, that we forget that the scene does nothing to move on the action of the play in a direct sense. One wonders how much more Osborne might have created from similarly based relationships in other plays, that between Redl and the Countess, for example, in *A Patriot for Me*, or between Pamela and Constance in *Time Present*.

We have insisted, at some length, that the quality of a play by Osborne derives from the depth of the hero's characterisation and from his rhetorical talents. One should also be aware of the fact that most of Osborne's plays are well enough constructed to be performed, if so desired, in a manner which gives them a very different stress. It is quite possible to see them through the eyes of the other characters. Ruth, for example, could offer an insight into the despair of George Dillon, perhaps Hudson into Bill Maitland's, or even the Countess into Redl's. There has been an actual production along these lines of *The Entertainer*, effected in Berlin by Hans Lietzau. In this, the centre of the stage was occupied by Archie's daughter, Jean. The play gained in unity, for Jean is almost ever-present, and the episodic nature of the play, when centred on Archie, is lost.

The philippics of the heroes provide the highlights of more conventional productions, for in them we witness the full range of Osborne's rhetorical gifts. The language of these speeches is an inductive one, in which Osborne expresses his opinions in his own medium. The language of the articulate hero is much more elaborate than that of the minor dialogue of the plays. There are two levels of speech, the common everyday speech of the minor characters which is basically deductive, and the great, inductive monologues of the central figures. The interest and intellect of the audience is more easily awakened by these vivid monologues than by ordinary dialogue. The response to these lengthy speeches is from the audience, or from the action of the play, but rarely from the minor characters. In this way the audience notice the void around the hero, and they hasten to fill it themselves.

Inarticulateness is the linguistic component of our human portion of suffering, but Osborne never makes his heroes inarticulate—if they are to protest to any effect they must do so with more style than we can muster for ourselves. The good talker has a prime place in the theatre, but if drama is concerned with contemporary issues, and if its aim is to explore those issues with any degree of consistency, then the language of the theatre should have some familiarity with the language of everyday life. This, Osborne understands. He translates the vocabulary and idioms of common conversation into the rhetorical power of his heroes. He does not lift the talk of the street directly on to the stage as Pinter does, but recreates that speech so that his heroes speak as we ourselves *would wish* to. They use the same words, the same colloquialisms, but to much greater effect. There is nothing remarkable about Luther's simile—"I'm blocked up like an old crypt"—but, who, amongst us would use such effective figuratives? With visual word pictures like these, Osborne gains an immediacy of thought and a compression of language which is unknown in everyday life.

One reason for this revival of common speech was that during the fifties the theatre ceased to belong almost entirely to the middle classes, losing much of its social status in the process. It also stopped being some form of escape or means of relaxation. It became much more an experience of communal participation which was and is quite rare in England. It also became concerned with life in all its various forms. The older middle-class playwrights knew how words *should* be used rather than how they *are* used. Their language was controlled and correct. Osborne does not make this mistake, for cool detached speech would not suit either his characters, or the content of his plays. He engages life at a critical level in his plays, and marries the language of everyday life to that of the theatre. When Jimmy Porter speaks he means so much more to us than if Osborne had used the language of Eliot or Fry, or even *us*. When Jimmy finds his wife's goodbye note, he reads it aloud, and then bursts out:

> JIMMY. Oh, how could she be so bloody wet! Deep loving need! She couldn't say "You rotten bastard! I hate your guts, I'm clearing out, and I hope you rot!" No, she has to make a polite, emotional mess out of it! Deep loving need!

I never thought she was capable of being as phoney as that!
What is that—a line from one of those plays you've been in?[3]

This final throw-away remark to Helena puts a finger for us
on the relevant point. His wife Alison uses the language of
polite, genteel drawing-room romance, a language totally
divorced from the facts of the Porter *ménage*. Jimmy's scorn
is immediate and real, his words are in step with his nature *and*
the situation. There is nothing forced or phoney—"that makes
me puke"—is only too real.

It is this innate ability of Osborne's to match language to
character which marks his plays so indelibly as his own. This
language is simple yet lyrical, contrived yet real. It is
theatrically thrilling, and if the dialogue of the minor characters
appears to be weak, might that not have been effected with the
deliberate purpose of focusing our attention upon the central
character. Had the "minor language" contained more substance, more argument, more invective, then our interest might
have been diverted from the all-consuming heroes. What
Osborne needed was to create plots of reasonable verisimilitude,
but which permitted the central character to legitimately express
his view within the action of that plot. Whilst these heroes are
unable to alter society, for the odds against them are too great
they dominate those around them, and this is only natural.
They themselves prevent any substantial minor dialogue
developing, for they are always interrupting, questioning,
rebuking, and inexorably giving their own opinion. It is the
strength of their feelings which charges the plays with
"electricity" and gives them so much impact. Jimmy's
incredulity at Alison's departure, Archie's breakdown during
his nun's story, Bill's panic when legal contacts refuse to speak
to him, Pamela's avoidance of an emotional scene with Murray
and Constance; in each, the private fear becomes at the same
time a public warning.

Osborne is not a didactic writer in the sense that he tries to
turn his characters into socialist lecturers, although in fact one
of them, Holyoake, is. He makes them believable human
beings, and puts them in credible situations. If we choose to

---

[3] *L.B.A.*, p. 36.

ignore the social or political implications of a play, we still have an effective drama. Osborne, knowing that his characters can never win their battle against society, spins a protective web around them, making a moral implicit rather than explicit, a hero human rather than symbolic. The heroes' failing is that they maintain idealistic purposes which are impossible to achieve, but their refusal to surrender to the social forces which threaten them is always plausible. Unless conditions are suitable (and they are not yet) ideals like theirs are meaningless in the practical sense. Such a high moral purpose endangers life, and ensures conflict and ultimate defeat. By witnessing the defeat of Osborne's heroes, we begin to question the means and ends of a society which ensures their failure. The playwright tries to impress his beliefs upon us within the action of his plays. If we recognised his principle as being substantially correct then he might well stir us to significant action; if on the other hand, we have rejected those principles, then he is more likely to arouse in us that hostility which his own characters seem to enjoy so much. In the sympathies and antipathies of a play we are able to make further refinements and definitions about ourselves, and about the playwright. We may feel ourselves into a play, or we may not. This accord will depend not only upon plot and character but upon thought and experience. The thought of a play will acquaint the spectator with what the playwright perceives as the forces which motivate men, and his view of the place of man in society and in the universe. Experience will condition whether we accept his view or reject it.

   We no longer live in a time when we recognise the inevitability of historical growth. The development of existentialism, whether the Christian form of Kierkegaard stressing the idea that in God, man may find freedom from tension, or Sartre's atheistic belief that man is alone in a Godless universe, and so needs to reject convention for the right of free determination, helped us transcend an attitude which accepted historical growth. What is needed, if morality is to be valid, is positive participation—and Osborne would be in full agreement with this. Yet he would not reject the historical approach entirely, for the sentimental longing which appears in his plays suggests that he would welcome some form of ensured stability, combined with that individual freedom stressed by Sartre's existentialism. Osborne is concerned with both the individual and society, he wishes to protect the individual's rights by urging society to adopt worthy ends. In a world of debased commercial values and mass standards, we can no longer rely on the old traditional integrated community to pass on the best values. Saving those values and society is a job for the minority, those with intelligence *and* sensibility. Of necessity they will find themselves cut off from their fellows, until "the donkeys are left behind because the other animals have learned to hear". Thus Osborne's heroes are determined to hang on grimly, for they are convinced they have the right values in a world which has accepted the wrong ones. Their eventual defeat simply reminds us how far we still have to go.

Osborne explores the state of "ennui" of people whose material aims have been fulfilled, but who, in the absence of other positive social ideals are bored and exasperated because of their fundamentally commercial outlook. These people become aware that their "humanness" demands more satisfaction, and Osborne sees his task to be the assertion of humanity in the face of whatever is threatening it. At the moment, that threat seems to be the wish of man "to enter the Great Washing Machine", as Christiane Rochefort so aptly put it. This is especially true of his last two plays which tackle the problems of public "success" as a threat to private integrity.

This concern of Osborne's is historically sound, for in the rush towards the climax of the socialist state, his own generation seems to have penalised the very people they set out to help. Osborne is not only aware of the direction in which society is moving, he is also aware that the twentieth century is full of self-blame, for it knows it has failed to provide man with a worthy ideal. In such a world man has relinquished his right to live *voluntarily* within society, he now submits fully to the collective will, and no longer even judges for himself. In contrast, Osborne's heroes *do* judge themselves right and society wrong. Hence the repetitiveness of the playwright's themes, principles reiterated time and again for fear that no one is listening. Osborne's task is to urge society towards fuller responsibility. He seeks a richer achievement for human beings and stresses the creative need. In a world where men no longer live co-operatively together but are reduced to negative conformity, he pleads that whilst his heroes may fail to change the world, at least their protest is valuable. The man in the street knows he cannot change the world so he accepts it. Osborne's *extra-ordinary* heroes believe they can alter it; when they realise they can't, should we condemn them for trying? There is surely a positive function in standing against the tide if one thinks that the current of events is moving in the wrong direction. With his vibrant rhetoric Osborne tries to arrest our blind headlong rush, and to make us aware of our futility:

> FRANK. They're all so busy, speeding down the middle of the road together, not giving a damn where they're going, as long as they're in the bloody middle! The rotten Bastards![4]

Only today are we beginning to live not by the rules which we inherit but by values which we discover for ourselves. Some of these new standards may even be anarchic but at least they allow humans to be themselves. We are gradually realising that our personal needs should be satisfied first. Osborne's protest aims at securing this end. Behind his open criticism lies a belief in a better world, and the hope that in that world humans will be allowed to live as *they* wish, and not as society requires them to live. The flag will not be kept flying at all costs, for it is only a symbol, and there are, after all, more worthwhile pursuits for thinking human beings.

We may interpret the plays, *A Patriot for Me* and *A Bond Honoured*, as evidence of a shift in emphasis by Osborne in the direction of self-realisation and self-acceptance. In the first, Alfred Redl struggles manfully with his latent homosexuality, trying to obey conventional dictates: finally he throws them aside to realise his true nature. In the latter play, Leonido is almost a projection of this self-realisation process, for he forms a bond which enables him to live solely for his own pleasure. By a pact with fate, he exchanges his afterlife for complete freedom here on earth. Osborne seems to suggest in these two plays that we might rid ourselves of many of our own anxieties and tensions if we too were to obey our own

[4] *E.*, p. 68.

nature and be true to our own desires, rather than conform to "acceptable behaviour". This represents a significant change in his attitude, for now he would have us listen to ourselves rather than to him. His heroes no longer seek to push their own personal guilt on to us as some form of collective social guilt. The free life would serve both as moral and example to us, the defeat of the hero should only spur us to further endeavour in this direction. There will always be a need for this kind of suggestive dissent in a society which is as integrated as ours.

Osborne's *For the Meantime* plays appear to represent a further refinement in his attitude, for in them his public anger has soured into bitter dissatisfaction. The characters in his latest two plays seem incapable of controlling their circumstances and need to reassure themselves endlessly. There is no Porter-like call to action, the only call is for another round of drinks. They do very little, having earned their freedom they wonder what to do with it. All they achieve is to air their guilt complexes, and hang-on and hope for something better to happen.

Osborne can no longer see any point in bemoaning the loss of our brave new causes, what is needed now is new thought and new hope. Thus we have reached a time for introspection. "We're all in the show-business now" but without confidence or ideals. Perhaps we shall seek again the standards of Gideon Orme and Billy Rice. Osborne's flirtation with the past has become a more serious affair. It is at this present time that our revaluation must be made and our need for encouragement acknowledged.

The most serious criticism of Osborne's work can be directed at these latest forms of protest and at his more common "angry" ones. Whilst Redl, Leonido, Pamela, and Laurie assert their right to be complete individuals, like all Osborne heroes they rarely attempt to amplify their values. Surely values which are passed on, need to be defined, rather than simply re-established or rejected? They also need to be shared, but Osborne never suggests how we should achieve these ends. We must obviously do something more positive than just save values for or from society. Osborne's failure to tackle this problem is probably due to the fact that he did not wish to overburden his plays with any additional intellectual content for fear of weakening their emotional appeal. We are never quite sure which values he wishes to retain and re-affirm, and which he would do away with and why. When one considers the ambiguous sentimentality which expresses itself in much of his work, then this omission is all the more regrettable.

Plays are works of art which also serve as a form of research into the life and times from which they grow. As long as they work in the theatre that is all that really matters, and we have constantly repeated that Osborne's do. The fancy labels, romanticist, naturalist, neo-realist, absurdist, factualist, will in time, pass. It is, however, always interesting to know where a play or movement originates, to examine the influences on it and its own influence on other movements. Strictly speaking, Osborne is much too individual to be classified as a member of any school, though he was, of course, branded as an "Angry Young Man"; we shall however attempt, albeit briefly, to "place" his work as far as contemporary post-war drama is concerned. Our statements will necessarily be generalisations stressing what various writers have in common rather than what differentiates them.

The first "angry" play was, in reality, *Ubu-Roi* by Alfred Jarry, produced in France in 1896 and recently revived at the Royal Court Theatre. The play opens with the exclamation "merdre", and is full of savage disdain, yet it was quickly forgotten as a trend-setter until the French theatrical revival of the nineteen-fifties. In the nineteen-thirties Antonin Artaud in his essays "Le Théâtre et son Double", stressed the importance of the theatre as a means of remedying the injustices and faults of society. His gift to drama was the theatre of cruelty, which aims to shock, to bring the public into contact with the real nature of existence. Thus there was an early movement away from the theatre of escape, and, after World War II, this new critical awareness formed itself into two distinct groups, the realists and the absurdists. Some playwrights, leaders of their own movements, such as Sartre, have certain affinities to both, but in general the realists have grouped themselves around the figure of the late Bertold Brecht, and the absurdists around Eugene Ionesco and Samuel Beckett.

The basic concept of the theatre of the absurd is the ridiculousness of modern existence. This is revealed by images which are in themselves absurd, a young man, for example, trying to teach a collection of weighing-machines to sing the Hallelujah Chorus. For the absurdist, a man has dignity if he is able to face reality in all its senselessness without illusion. There is no God and no meaning in the progress of man from birth to death. This belief is intellectual, anarchic, and pessimistic. It repudiates logic, psychological consistency or any commitments to ideals. It rejects absolutely, social and political change or improvement. The absurdist concentrates on a world in which communication has ceased, he does not make a statement but asks a question. That question is: once our basic needs are satisfied, what is the point? The consequences for the theatre of such a negative belief are important. By extension we should get, if it were possible, no action, no characters, no dialogue—the ultimate masterpiece must be a solitary spotlight on an empty stage. In practice, the more common ingredients of drama are replaced, by various visual devices, symbolic scenery, fragmentary dialogue, and negative themes. The absurd theatre claims to have a therapeutic effect on its audience. It has developed in three reasonably distinct directions. It is strongest in France where the intellect is still admired, and the leading exponents are Ionesco and Beckett. In America it has evolved into the black comedy typified in the work of Jones and Kopit. In Britain it has been more or less diluted, appearing in the work of playwrights such as Shaffer and Simpson.

In opposition to the theatre of the absurd, we have the neo-realist movement, posthumously headed by Bertold Brecht, who derived his epic theatre from the works of Ibsen, Strindberg, and Büchner. Brecht's theatre is essentially rational and assumes that men have definite motives, if only those of self-interest. Its basic assumption is that talk about ideals is wasted until bellies are filled. Brecht finds the key to man's soul in his social and political environment, and assumes that communication is possible between human beings. His appeal is not to the emotion but to the intellect, yet he often wrote with the poetic ambiguity of the artist. The most marked and lasting characteristic of this epic theatre is the "verfremdungseffekt"—the alienation effect. These attempts to alienate by means of technical devices an audience's emotional involvement in a play. It encourages detached thought, permitting the spectator to investigate a view of man in the world as it confronts him. In order to achieve this effect Brecht evolved the epic narrative, a loose sequence of scenes strung together, but with each existing as an entity in its own right. Brecht discouraged hero worship and many of his central characters are presented in a deliberately ambiguous way. His productions were avowedly theatrical, almost medieval in presentation. He believed quite simply in plain reality and sought a method whereby the normal everyday economic process could be effectively dramatised. He opposed naturalistic acting, because for him it was a return to the theatre of escape. He refused to permit actors to identify with their parts, believing that the human condition is not fixed but depends on circumstances and time. Brecht's theatre explores humanity itself and not the romantic individualist. His iconoclastic attitude and vigorous experiment served to break down many established theatrical conventions and this feat may well be his most lasting gift to the art of modern drama. His empirical attitude has had a valuable influence on the work of Arden, Bolt, Kops, and Whiting, as well as on the production techniques of Joan Littlewood. Brecht's technical influence on Osborne has been basically unimportant as we have explained elsewhere. The epic frame-works of *The Entertainer* and *Luther* served not to alienate but to encourage the audience's involvement. If we consider motivation, then the two playwrights are much closer in attitude, for they both believe in a rational communicative man, and both are committed to social and political change. Osborne has gone further than Brecht by putting his faith in man's emotion—feel now, think later.

Of the post-war American playwrights, Arthur Miller and Tennessee Williams have probably had the greatest direct influence on contemporary British theatre. In their turn, many American playwrights, such as Albee, Kopit, Jones, and Gelber, have been influenced by European realism, and also by the reappearance of the theatre of cruelty.

Osborne acknowledges some influence by Tennessee

Williams, for he believes that the American playwright helped condition British audiences to appreciate plays which deal realistically with life. Williams is, in fact, a poet disguised as a dramatist. His plays are full of romance and protest and an angry naturalism pervades them. He is fond of extremes and earthy situations, and we can see Osborne's esteem for Williams in the playwrights' mutual desire to engage life "where it hurts". But in truth, Williams is very parochial, his image is that of the South, and his plays contain little which is relevant to either the British temperament or theatrical scene. In some way, Williams may have influenced Osborne and others regarding the non-deification of the female, but otherwise his influence on British drama has been slight.

Arthur Miller is a much more didactic writer than Williams, and is similar in style to Arnold Wesker. His protest is a political one and his concern is with power and freedom. Miller's targets are much more grandiose than Osborne's, who remains more concerned with the antagonism between classes, and everyday social attitudes. There is, however, some affinity, especially in theme, for both wish to provide a better world, and both are concerned that British drama should not become, as Miller once thought it might, "hermetically sealed off from real life".

The realists have had a much greater influence on British post-war drama than the absurdists, for in general British dramatists see themselves as artists who have more than a passive role to fill in society. They would grant that so far no philosophy or ideology has cured man's pain or anxiety, but this does not mean that we should stop trying, as the absurdists suggest. Osborne would never be content to shut himself up in the tower of solipsism—indeed when his form of protest is absent from society the line between how life should be and how life is, is desperately thin. Osborne has created a compromise between the realist and the absurdist schools by combining the rational communicative society of the former with the concern for the individual of the latter. At the same time, his own originality and talent, given the conditions existing in Great Britain, have turned this compromise into a very personal concept.

Osborne's most original contribution to British drama may be summed up by the word "love". Love was a word only mentioned "lightly" in the theatre before the appearance of *Look Back in Anger*; it had rarely been present as an open problem. For Osborne, the love between man and woman, and the love between man and society, creates situations worth exploring, and in this play he tackled them. We see in it the various intensities of love—Jimmy's compulsive physical desire for Alison, his affection for his friend Cliff, his tender care for the old woman, his need to dominate Helena, and above all his general love for humanity, a feeling which finds expression in his disgust with his fellows for their willingness to accept second best. When faced with the placid half-living of the masses, Osborne's emotional wobble becomes visible, and his love turns to anger, almost hate. Without love we are nothing. In *The Entertainer*, Archie Rice tells us he is dead behind the eyes, yet we know he is not, he still seeks affection. Accustomed to denial, he steels himself against rebuff, and sings:

> ARCHIE. Why should I care
> Why should I let it touch me. . . .[5]

Behind this brave face his need for love becomes even more obvious, he asks the audience for the response he is unable to find in his domestic life, yet even in his final defeat he staggers off-stage to seek solace in the arms of his wife, Phoebe.

Osborne's plays cannot be divorced from their time, yet their message is universal, and in an amorphous society such as ours all the more significant. The emotional disease of England is apathy, and Osborne's real merit lies in his willingness to do battle with this deadening inertia. Osborne is, in fact, passionately devoted to England. By attempting to revive a tired population, he, and other writers of a like mind created a literary breakthrough in the 1950s. They added a special local note of protest to the general world-wide movement which sought a rational approach to human problems. The all-over-the-target radicalism of the British group gained for them the immediate force of expression which was needed to render their protest effective. At the same time, this lack of direction movingly

[5] *Op. cit.*, p. 24.

expressed their excess of love. None of their themes were new, the threat of isolation, the revolt against authority, the inadequacy of their own generation, all had been tackled before. The group's originality lay in the emotional force with which they made their protest. The determination to fight and to love was expressed in a compelled language, massively persuasive. Society could not fail to take notice.

It was the impact of Osborne's first play which established this movement. His drama is one which, whilst sentimental in parts, is more urgently connected with British contemporary life than either the absurdists or epic-realists will ever be. Osborne's output has been enormous, thirteen plays in twelve years, and few modern British dramatists escape his influence. His various qualities have been diversified, and then, as it were, more fully developed. In the work of Jellicoe, Mortimer, and Orton, Osborne's humour is extended. Delaney, Howarth, and Lynne, become more lyrical. His political awareness is reflected in Bolt, Chilton, and Whiting. Arden and Cooper expand the intellectual appeal. Osborne's realism is emphasised by the plays of Kops, Wesker, and Wood. His "absurd" concern with the individual, by Saunders and Simpson. Only Pinter, with his own originality, belief, and language, stands truly outside the sphere of Osborne's influence. Many foreign playwrights appear to be even more Osbornian than our own, Claus, Gelber, and Schisgal, for example.

None of these dramatists have matched "under one roof" the complex of talents which went into the construction of such outstanding plays as *Look Back in Anger*, *The Entertainer*, and *Inadmissible Evidence*. Osborne has given a recharge to Jarry's anger, related this to contemporary life, and combined it with a love for humanity. To realise this creation in the theatre, he has extended the language of ordinary life into his own particular form of rhetoric. Society will always need dissent, and if that dissension grows from a positive concern for value then it is all the more useful. Osborne is a man of strong convictions and he has never been afraid to state them, or to demonstrate his beliefs in his chosen medium, the theatre. His work is provocatively honest. His plays are experiments, and experiment means asking questions, it does not mean finding or giving answers.

By the force of his heroes' expressions, Osborne has stimulated society—he asks that we keep our grip, however tenuous, on life. He demands that we control our own destiny and do not relinquish our rights, individually or collectively. It is a worthy and serious motive.

N

Appendix A

FIRST PERFORMANCES

8 May 1956   *Look Back in Anger* at the Royal Court directed by Tony Richardson with Kenneth Haigh and Alan Bates.

10 Apr. 1957   *The Entertainer* at the Royal Court directed by Tony Richardson with Sir Laurence Olivier and Brenda de Banzie.

11 Feb. 1968   *Epitaph for George Dillon* at the Royal Court directed by William Gaskill with Robert Stephens.

14 Apr. 1959   *The World of Paul Slickey* at the Pavilion, Bournemouth, directed by John Osborne with Dennis Lotis.

6 Nov. 1960   *A Subject of Scandal and Concern* televised by the B.B.C., directed by Tony Richardson with Richard Burton.

26 Jun. 1961   *Luther* at the Theatre Royal, Nottingham, directed by Tony Richardson with Albert Finney.

19 Jul. 1962   "Plays for England" at the Royal Court. *The Blood of the Bambergs* directed by John Dexter with John Meillon. *Under Plain Cover* directed by Jonathon Miller with Anton Rodgers and Ann Beach.

9 Sep. 1964   *Inadmissible Evidence* at the Royal Court directed by Anthony Page with Nicol Williamson.

30 Jun. 1965   *A Patriot for Me* at the Royal Court. The English Stage Society by arrangement with The English Stage Company. Directed by Anthony Page with Maximilian Schell.

6 Jun. 1966   *A Bond Honoured* at the National Theatre directed by John Dexter with Robert Stephens.

23 May 1968   *Time Present* at the Royal Court directed by Anthony Page with Jill Bennett.

3 Jul. 1968   *The Hotel in Amsterdam* at the Royal Court directed by Anthony Page with Paul Scofield.

Appendix B

AN OSBORNE SYMPOSIUM 1966

The Management of the Royal Court Theatre, on the occasion of the 10th Anniversary of the opening of *Look Back in Anger*, 8 May, 1956, at that theatre, asked a number of prominent theatrical figures to estimate Osborne's significance in the British theatre. Some replies:

"John Osborne didn't contribute to the British theatre: he set off a land-mine called *Look Back in Anger* and blew most of it up. The bits have settled back into place, of course, but it can never be the same again." ALAN SILLITOE.

"Long before Oedipus there were Oedipus complexes, long before Hamlet there were gloomy Danes. But the day the figure took shape in a poet's mind, the day he got a name, the world acquired a new reference. It need not have happened. The right imagination isn't always there. John Osborne's achievement is that one day he gave form where no one else saw that form lay. But I hate the word achievement. John Osborne is also impatient, restless, courageous and colossally talented. It is his potential today that matters even more." PETER BROOK.

"John Osborne's passion saved the English theatre from death through gentility. At a time of uncertain and hovering formal experiment, he has shown that the conventional theatre can still extend its emotional and verbal range beyond what we had any of us hoped. But above all, in an age when the conventional pay lip-service to humanism, he has challenged humanistic hypocrisies by demanding and obtaining a complex compassion for a wide range of the least lovable, least cosy and least glamorous of human beings." ANGUS WILSON.

"A theatre that wishes to stay alive needs passion and contemporary relevance (sometimes known, sneeringly, as 'effemeral journalism'). Elegance, good taste and verbal mellifluence, though excellent qualities in themselves, are inadequate substitutes. John Osborne supplied the missing ingredients at a time when it seemed that their absence was no longer even noticed." JOHN ARDEN.

N*

" 'We owe so much to you' " Staupitz tells Luther in the last act of John's play. We all do. John Osborne brought back honour, substance and dignity to a theatre which had been fed for decades on 'shells for shells, empty things for empty men'. John was the first, the breakthrough of the dramatists who have crowded in since 1956. But their breakthrough could only have happened by the authority and humanity of his voice. He is unique and alone in his ability to put on the stage the quick of himself, his pain, his squalor, his nobility—terrifyingly alone." TONY RICHARDSON.

Bibliography

I. Works by John Osborne

a. Texts

All plays are published by Faber and Faber, who also published Osborne's script for the film *Tom Jones*. In the United States, the plays are published by Criterion Books. *Epitaph for George Dillon*, which he wrote in collaboration with Anthony Creighton, is also available in Penguin (New English Dramatists No. 2).

Look Back in Anger (1957).
The Entertainer (1957).
Epitaph for George Dillon (1958).
The World of Paul Slickey (1959).
Luther (1961).
Plays for England (1963):
 The Blood of the Bambergs;
 Under Plain Cover.

Inadmissible Evidence (1965).
A Patriot for Me (1966).
A Bond Honoured (1966).
Time Present (1968).
The Hotel in Amsterdam (1968).

b. Writings

"The Writer in His Age", reply to questionnaire by *London Magazine*, April 1957.
"They Call it Cricket", *Declaration*, ed. T. Masschler. London, 1957.
"The Epistle to the Philistines", in *Tribune*, 13 May 1960.
"That Awful Museum", in *Twentieth Century*, February 1961.
"A Letter to My Fellow Countrymen", in *Tribune*, 18 Aug. 1961.
"On Critics and Criticism", in *Sunday Telegraph*, 28 Aug. 1966.
Interview with Kenneth Tynan in *The Observer*, 7 July 1968.

II. Criticism

a. Books

ALLSOP, K. *The Angry Decade*. London (Owen) 1968.
The Beat Generation, eds. G. Feldman and M. Gartenberg. New York (Citadel) 1958.
BRADBROOK, M. C. *English Dramatic Form*. London (Chatto & Windus) 1965.
BRUSTEIN, R. *The Theatre of Revolt*. London (Methuen) 1962.

CHIARI, J.   *Landmarks of Contemporary Drama*. New York (Jenkins) 1965.
COE, R. *Ionesco*. Edinburgh (Oliver & Boyd) 1961.
Declaration, ed. T. Masschler. London (MacGibbon & Kee) 1957.
ERIKSON E. H.   *Young Man Luther*. 1959.
ESSLIN, M.   *The Theatre of The Absurd*. London (Eyre & Spottiswoode)
    1961.
Experimental Drama, ed. W. Armstrong. London (Bell) 1963.
FINDLATER, R.   *The Future of the Theatre*. London (Fabian Society) 1959.
GRAY, R.   *Brecht*. Edinburgh (Oliver & Boyd) 1962.
HALL, W. AND WATERHOUSE, K.   *Writers Theatre*. London (Heine-
    mann) H.E.B. Paperback, 1968.
KERSHAW, J.   *The Present Stage*. London (Fontana) 1966.
KICHEN, L.   *Mid-Century Drama*. London (Faber) 1960.
Look Back in Anger: A Selection of Critical Essays, ed. J. R. Taylor. London
    (Macmillan) 1968.
LUMLEY, F.   *Trends in Twentieth-Century Drama*, London (Barrie &
    Rockliff) 1967.
MAGEE, B.   *The New Radicalism*. London (Secker & Warburg) 1962.
MANDER, J.   *The Writer and His Commitment*. London (Secker &
    Warburg) 1961.
MONTGOMERY, J.   *The Fifties*. London (Allen & Unwin) 1965.
MORRIS, J.   *The Outsiders*. London (Faber) 1963.
NICOLL, A.   *British Drama*. London (Harrap) 1962.
SISSONS, M. AND FRENCH, P.   *The Age of Austerity*. London (Hodder &
    Stoughton) 1963.
TAYLOR, J. R.   *Anger and After*. Harmondsworth (Penguin) Pelican
    Books, 1963.
TYNAN, K.   *Tynan on Theatre*. Harmondsworth (Penguin) Pelican Books,
    1964.
VAN DE PERRE, H.   *John Osborne—boze jonge man*. The Hague (Lannoo)
    1962.
WARD, A.   *Twentieth-Century English Literature*. London (Methuen) 1964.
WYATT, W.   *Distinguished for Talent*. London (Hutchinson) 1965.

b. *Magazines and Periodicals*

ANDERSON, L.   "Stand up, Stand up!" in *Sight and Sound*, Autumn 1961.
BEAUFORT, JOHN.   "Second Play by Osborne Reaches U.S.", in *The
    Christian Science Monitor*, 24 Feb. 1958.
BEAVAN, JOHN.   "Unlucky Jim", in *The Twentieth Century*, July 1956.
BRIEN, ALAN.   "Broken Mould", in *The Spectator*, 21 Feb. 1958.
BRUSTEIN, ROBERT.   "Theatre Chronicle", in *Hudson Review*, Spring
    1959.
BRYDEN, RONALD.   "Osborne at the Ball", in *New Statesman*, 9 Jul. 1965.
Christian Century.   "A Layman's Guide to Recent Religious Trends:
    Osborne's Luther", 30 Oct. 1963.
CLURMAN, HAROLD.   "Theatre", in *The Nation*, 1 Mar. 1958.

CLURMAN, HAROLD. "Theatre", in *The Nation*, 19 Oct. 1963.
——. "Plays and Politics", in *The Nation*, 25 Oct. 1965.
DENTY, VERA D. "The Psychology of Martin Luther", in *The Catholic World*, November 1961.
DUPREY, RICHARD A. AND PALMS, CHARLES L. "Luther", *The Catholic World*, November 1963.
ELLIOT, GEORGE P. "Letter from London", in *The Nation*, 30 Dec. 1961.
FINDLATER, RICHARD. "No Time for Tragedy", in *The Twentieth Century*, January 1957.
GASCOIGNE, BAMBER. "First Person Singular", in *Spectator*, 4 Aug. 1961.
——. "From the Head", in *Spectator*, 27 Jul. 1962.
GASSNER, JOHN. "Broadway in Review", in *Educational Theatre Journal*, December 1963.
GIBBS, W. "Two Very Sad Young Men", in *The New Yorker*, 12 Oct. 1957.
GILLIATT, PENELOPE. "People Are Talking About . . .", in *Vogue*, 1 Apr. 1957.
——. "People Are Talking About . . .", in *Vogue*, 1 Feb. 1958.
GILMAN, RICHARD. "The Stage: John Osborne's Luther", in *The Commonweal*, 18 Oct. 1963.
GROSS, JOHN. "The Culture Mongers", in *Vogue*, 1 Mar. 1962.
——. "1793 and All That", in *Encounter*, November 1964.
GROSS, JOHN. "Rebels and Renegades", in *Encounter*, October 1965.
HANCOCK, ROBERT. "Anger", in *Spectator*, 5 Apr. 1957.
HARTLEY, ANTHONY. "Angry Romantic", in *Spectator*, 18 May 1956.
HATCH, ROBERT. "Theatre", in *The Nation*, 22 Nov. 1958.
HEWES, HENRY. "Castles May Crumble", in *The Saturday Review*, 13 Oct. 1956.
——. "Fifteen Turns in the Theatre Real", in *The Saturday Review*, 11 May 1957.
——. "Sir Archie Rice", in *The Saturday Review*, 1 Mar. 1958.
——. "The 'Cad' as Hero", in *The Saturday Review*, 22 Nov. 1958.
——. "Overdoers Undone", in *The Saturday Review*, 12 Oct. 1963.
——. "Unsentimental Journeys", in *The Saturday Review*, 29 May 1965.
——. "England's Summer Season", in *The Saturday Review*, 14 Aug. 1965.
——. "Angry Middle-Aged Man", in *The Saturday Review*, 18 Dec. 1965.
——. "Unsubmissive Performance", in *The Saturday Review*, 8 Jan. 1966.
HOLLAND, MARY. "Vogue's Eye View", in *Vogue*, 1 Mar. 1962.
HOLLIS, CHRISTOPHER. "Keeping Up With The Rices", in *Spectator*, 18 Oct. 1957.
JONES, D. A. N. "Hot Thing", in *New Statesman*, 17 Jun. 1966.
LAMBERT, J. W. "Plays in Performance", in *Drama*, Autumn 1961.
LARDNER, JOHN. "An Artist and a Sadist", in *The New Yorker*, 15 Nov. 1958.
LEWIS, THEOPHILUS. "Luther", in *America*, 26 Oct. 1963.
——. "Reviewer's Notebook", in *America*, 21 Jul. 1962.
Life. "Snarling Success: A Biting and Entertaining Play, Look Back in Anger, Sets Broadway Ablaze", 14 Oct. 1957.

The London Magazine. "The Writer in His Age: John Osborne", April 1957.

MAROWITZ, C. "The Ascension of John Osborne", in *Tulane Drama Review*, VII, Winter 1962.

MCCARTEN, JOHN. "Contumacious Theologican", in *The New Yorker*, 5 Oct. 1963.

——. "A Long, Long Wail A-Winding", in *The New Yorker*, 11 Dec. 1965.

MCCARTHY, MARY. "Odd Man In", in *Partisan Review*, Winter 1959.

MORGAN, E. "That Uncertain Feeling", in *Encore*, 1958.

Newsweek. "On a Rowdy Adventure", 24 Feb. 1958.

——. "The 'Hero' Is a Heel", 17 Nov. 1958.

——. "The Two Luthers", 7 Oct. 1963.

——. "A Man for These Times", 13 Dec. 1965.

The New Yorker. "The Talk of the Town: Good-Natured Man", 26 Oct. 1957.

——. "The Talk of the Town: Notes and Comment", 8 Oct. 1966.

PANTER-DOWNES, MOLLIE. "Letter from London", in *The New Yorker*, 28 Sep. 1957.

——. "Letter from London", in *The New Yorker*, 14 Oct. 1961.

——. "Letter from London", in *The New Yorker*, 17 Apr. 1965.

PRIDEAUX, TOM. "Narcissus Spitting at His Own Image", in *Life*, 14 Jan. 1966.

PRITCHETT, V. S. "Operation Osborne", in *New Statesman*, 4 Aug. 1961.

PRYCE-JONES, ALAN. "New York Openings: Luther", in *Theatre Arts*, December 1963.

RAYMOND, JOHN. "A Look Back at Mr Osborne", in *New Statesman*, 19 Jan. 1957.

——. "Mid-Century Blues", in *New Statesman*, 12 Oct. 1957.

RUPP, GORDON E. "John Osborne and the Historical Luther", in *The Expository Times*, February 1962.

——. "Luther and Mr Osborne". *Cambridge Quarterly*, Vol. 1, Number 1.

RUTHERFORD, MALCOLM. "Osborne's Language", in *Spectator*, 18 Sep. 1964.

SHEED, WILFRID. "The Stage: Johnny One Note", in *The Commonweal*, 24 Dec. 1965.

SCOTT, J. D. "Britain's Angry Young Men", in *The Saturday Review*, 27 Jul. 1957.

SIMON, JOHN. "Theatre Chronicle", in *The Hudson Review*, Winter 1963-4.

SONTAG, SUSAN. "Going to the Theatre", in *Partisan Review*, Winter 1964.

Theatre Arts. "On Broadway: Look Back in Anger", December 1957.

——. "On Broadway: The Entertainer", April 1958.

——. "Play Reviews: Alan Pryce-Jones at the Theatre", March 1961.

THESPIS. "Theatre Notes", in *English*, Summer 1958.

——. "Theatre Notes", in *English*, Spring 1962.

Time. "The Most Angry Fella", 22 Apr. 1957.

——. "Lucky Jim and His Pals", 27 May 1957.

——. "New Plays in Manhattan", 14 Oct. 1957.

Time. "New Plays in Manhattan", 17 Nov. 1958.
——. "A Good-Intoxicated Man", 4 Oct. 1963.
——. "Hell's Isolation Ward", 10 Dec. 1965.
TREWIN, J. C. "A Tale of Three Nights", in *The Illustrated London News*, 27 Apr. 1957.
——. "The Latest Immortals", in *The Illustrated London News*, 28 Sep. 1957.
——. "A Word in the Ear", in *The Illustrated London News*, 12 Aug. 1961.
——. "Hit or Miss", in *The Illustrated London News*, 4 Aug. 1962.
——. "Sound and Fury", in *The Illustrated London News*, 26 Sep. 1964.
WATT, DAVID. "Coming Unstuck", in *Spectator*, 19 Apr. 1957.
WEBSTER, MARGARET. "A Look at the London Season", in *Theatre Arts*, May 1957.
WEISS, SAMUEL A. "Osborne's Angry Young Play", in *Educational Theatre Journal*, December 1960.
WESKER, ARNOLD. "Centre 42: The Secret Reins", in *Encounter*, March 1962.
WHITING, JOHN. "Luther", in *London Magazine*, October 1961.
WORSLEY, T. C. "A Test Case", in *The New Statesman and Nation*, 19 May 1965.
——. "Minority Culture", in *The New Statesman and Nation*, 26 Jan. 1957.
——. "Cut and Come Again", in *The New Statesman and Nation*, 20 Apr. 1957.
——. "England, Our England!", in *New Statesman*, 21 Sep. 1957.

Index